MY SOULMATE
MY LOVE
MY NARCISSIST

Healing and Recovery from a Narcissistic Relationship

By Dr. Bindu Babu, I-MD, PHD

DEDICATION

I dedicate this book to people all over the world who suffer in silence and isolation. May their spirits find fortitude by the voices of others who were able to share their stories.

I also dedicate this book to my children for the incredible passion they instill within my heart.

TABLE OF CONTENTS

ACKNOWLEDGEMENTS

ACKNOWLEDGMENTS

*The greatest beauty is that of one making life
beautiful for another...*

Thank you ~ Linda Vettrus-Nichols & Terry Earthwind Nichols

INTRODUCTION

Life is meant to be lived in happiness. It's a journey designed to be filled with love, joy, abundance, and most importantly... fulfilling your purpose. Every one of us has the inner strength and the mending ability to bring forth the positive.

Narcissistic abuse doesn't just happen suddenly or overnight. It creeps up until one day you don't even recognize yourself. It's slowly dehumanizing. You lose your identity, self-esteem, and confidence where you become an empty shell of yourself.

The reality is that you can recover and reclaim that strong, independent, powerful person you truly are. You can find your own sense of contentment from a place of self-love and inner healing.

This book will empower you to understand and change your circumstances. As well as to heal what is needed so you can move forward on a positive path of growth and well-being.

If a narcissist enters your life, especially in the form of a romantic partner, they will completely drain you of your entire sense of self. When you finally break free, you'll find yourself starting over from scratch – questioning everything you thought you knew about yourself.

Even though we can't fix the past we can definitely work together to understand the challenges we are facing today and resolve them in order to live a more fulfilling life. Having structured tools, we can learn to trust our instincts. This will bring forth self-empowerment so we can follow through with our vision.

Through my personal journey and the circumstances that were occurring in my life, including narcissistic abuse, I learned to love myself.

Being a Medical Physician, I was too left brained to accept my intuitive abilities. I looked at it as luck or coincidence. I couldn't see past anything without a scientific basis. Eventually as my life rolled out in front of me, I learned there is much more to life than just science.

Due to my journey of narcissistic relationships I learned about sustainable healing, mindset, and various Quantum modalities. I have worked and been mentored by some of the great healers of our time, Dr. Brian Weiss MD, Dr. Paul Drouin MD, Dr Amit Goswami, and Dr. Bruce Lipton. It has been a privilege and an attribute to my life purpose to passionately support others on their healing journey.

Today I am an Integrative Physician, Quantum Based Transformational Life Coach, Past Life Regression Therapist, and Intuitive Reiki Master where I work with clients all over the world. I am here to guide my clients to heal and leave their past where it belongs so they can lead a life of fulfillment and happiness.

An Open Letter to My Narcissist

All I ever learned was to give love and you taught me how to hate.

The beauty you tried so hard to show me... the colors of the world as you called it... were delivered as promised, except I did not know I was to learn the colors of all your haunting shadows.

I tried so hard for the both of us as I did understand the pain of your soul. I thought I could save you, save us... but little did I know the blindness of my unwavering faith in human kindness was the weapon that would be used against me in your darkest moments.

Where the impossible of the hurts, you made possible which no human deserves. The eruption of your anger, the turmoil along with the beautiful dreams, spun me in confusion that gripped the very essence of my being.

The spirit of never giving up on a loved one, the sacrament of marriage, my children, society, my family, and judgement was the very weapon I used against myself.

What I did understand, despite all your love, all the forgiveness, the confusion, the challenges, was... you're selfish and willing to destroy anything in your path once triggered. That's a battle that I choose to let go.

So, thank you. Thank you for the life lesson. Thank you for opening me up to the strong woman I never knew was inside me, as I would not be who I am today without you.

I continue my journey filled with so much love.

Letting go of the hate that you taught me.

LOVE IS POWERFUL

We all come across that one person who takes our breath away. You know the one that shows us the sun, moon, and stars? In fact, he would go get the moon for us if he could. It's everything that we ever hear about in a Nicholas Sparks' movie. That person who makes you the center of *their* universe. Showering you with such love and devotion that you are sure you just died and met your soulmate from heaven. Like pinch me, this is too good to be true.

Soulmates

You look around and you see that no one else seems to have this type of connection with their partner. In fact, you just know that no one else could possibly be having this same experience. You are the only one having this deep connection with your dreamy new person. It's special, it's unique. You can see that this is different, and you tell yourself how damn lucky you are to have found him.

After all, we did grow up watching Cinderella. She was nothing but a poor rag girl who only had the kindness of her heart to offer. That was all the prince wanted. He wanted her and no one else. She was special.

He searched desperately through all his lands, holding fast to her glass slipper. All he wanted to do was to find her. This one single girl was the love of his life. He only wanted her.

Dreamy, isn't it? Sure. In reality, this is just a fairytale. Then one day the fairytale becomes true for you. You meet your prince charming. Just like in Cinderella, your prince leaves his castle to find you. In fact, he chases you with all his amazing charm. He acts like he can't live without you. Out of everyone in the world, he chooses you and you feel special. The slipper fits. Not only does it fit, it's Gucci.

Wake Up Call Number 1

Now it's only been about 2 days or 2 months and you are already talking about your future together. It's a short period of time. You know this isn't the norm or the social protocol, I mean *what will people think or say?* Oh, what the hell, you've got this. You know what you both have. You move in together and start planning your wedding.

Wake Up Call Number 2

Everything is going perfect. Then things start to change. It's subtle. Everything he once admired about you and appreciated becomes the epitome of your flaws. The dress you used to wear that he considered sexy, has become *in his mind* too short and whore-like. The once admired trait of you being a friendly extrovert has now become, *in his mind*, attention seeking behavior to lure men into your claws. The barbeque that you don't even recall attending is being used to let you know how you were flirting with Bob whom you don't even recall meeting.

Wake Up Call Number 3

As weeks or months or even years go by... you hang on for dear life... afraid to move right or left because you're afraid to upset or provoke him. You're gripped by the fear of losing this person. The all-consuming love you have for him becomes an obsession. It consumes you despite being belittled, criticized, devalued, and dismissed. You're doing everything you can to save the relationship. Your only focus is to bring back those love filled happy moments, the good times, where you were the center of his universe, when you were perfect in his eyes, which made him happy.

Wake Up Call Number 4

The perfect devotion that you used to receive from him is gone. It's replaced with constant criticism. Nothing you do is right. So much mistrust. You naively put forth more effort and exert yourself to give constant communication. It just doesn't work. You put in more effort to love harder, almost smothering to prove yourself and your worth. When you do finally master one of the qualities he has set forth, the rules change... and he will find something else disappointing about you. You're desperately doing your best to save the relationship. You know he loves you. Deep down inside you can feel his soul and your connection. He is your soulmate, and yet he punishes you for being too weak to love him.

Wake Up Call Number 5

Some days go well, and things are fine even magical. Then something else upsets him and he gets angry. The fights start up again and along with them comes unprecedented anger and even rage. Reality starts becoming warped and distorted. You start becoming a shell of yourself. *You stop talking to friends and family because you become convinced that something is wrong with you.* You believe that it's your doing that things aren't going well. In other words, everything is your fault.

Sound familiar?

Welcome to the world of narcissistic abuse. Hundreds of women and men all around the world have been through this type of toxicity.

Now a perception and question may arise from you: How could this be toxic abuse? You'll most likely answer your own question with: This isn't abuse. This is love. A love that has misunderstandings where I know my partner has great potential. There is a side of him only I know, only I can recognize and understand. A side he does not show anyone else but me. I know he truly loves me. I can help him and us. He will change.

Yes, all of this might be true.

It also doesn't mean that your partner isn't a Narcissist.

Abuse

Abuse comes in many forms, not just physical. Mental abuse is both psychological and emotional. Unlike physical abuse where you can see the bruises on a person, in mental abuse there are unseen wounds that run deep into the core of a person's being.

Narcissistic Abuse

As I mentioned in the introduction, narcissistic abuse doesn't just happen suddenly or overnight. It creeps up so slowly until one day you don't even recognize yourself. It's slowly dehumanizing. You lose your identity, self-esteem, and confidence. You try to make sense and comprehend your partner's behavior. You believe that if you put more effort into showing loyalty and honesty things will change. You know that if you just tried harder to be good enough, supportive enough, pretty enough, and sexy enough things will work out.

Wakeup Call Number 6

Instead of just pulling back from family and friends, you start to cut ties with the ones he despises, even though you know that you will be further isolated. You know you will be alone. You know you will only have him to turn to: The love of your life who has repeatedly hurt you. Betrayed you. Humiliated you with slander. Called you all sorts of obscenities in public displays of outrage. For example, when you were made the star of the show in front of everyone at your best friend's engagement party.

The secrets you had entrusted to him are now being used as weapons of cruelty. But you don't care. You still cut ties with family and friends in hopes that despite his apathy towards you, somewhere inside his angry self, love will emerge and shine upon you once again. This way you can get your beautiful dreamy life back. You just know it. The happiness that you both shared in the beginning will return, and finally you will regain stability.

Wakeup Call Number 7

The problem is that the narcissist will always find something new to cripple you, to devalue you.

They'll find something to feel disappointed about you and blame you for everything that is wrong. No matter how hard you try, you just can't measure up to their expectations.

You just want stability. At this point you may not have any self-esteem left to question their behavior. You may not even find a reason for the horrific rage that comes out of them or the ghosting.

You don't even know what hit you.

You are so dejected that you may even decide to shut down in silence as it's much easier to deal with than to receive their extreme unwarranted torture and wrath.

It's a constant teetering between having them love you wholeheartedly and the next minute hating the very essence of your being. This is what's so confusing. Then when you do decide to walk away, the tearful apologies and the love filled grandiose promises come pouring out. *You want to believe them, despite all the red flags screaming in your face and gut.*

You want to believe them so badly that the door opens, and the devil's dance begins once again.

NARCISSISTIC PERSONALITY DISORDER

In today's millennial world, the word narcissist is loosely thrown around. Anyone who we feel is utterly vain or full of themselves by taking their 500 social media selfies in one sitting is called a narcissist. *These aren't the people you need to worry about.* Even though they may seem to act like a narcissist, they are not one. *Being entitled or vain are traits seen in a narcissist, and yet that alone does not make them one.*

The term Narcissist means *a person who has Narcissistic Personality Disorder (NPD)* which is defined by The Mayo Clinic as "a mental disorder in which people have an inflated sense of their own importance and a deep need for admiration. Those with narcissistic personality disorder believe that they are superior to others and have little regard for other people's feelings. *But behind this mask of ultra-confidence lies a fragile self-esteem, vulnerable to the slightest criticism.*"

Narcissists have an exaggerated sense of self-importance and entitlement. There's a famous joke where a narcissist will be speaking to someone about himself/herself then pauses and says, "Well enough about me, how do you feel about me?" It all comes down to their validation, attention, and serious need for affirmation. That's how a narcissist feeds their ego. It's their survival technique.

They are in love with this inflated self-image because it allows them to avoid their deep feelings of insecurity.

Anything or anyone can easily rattle this insecurity because narcissists are extremely sensitive. They react immaturely to the slightest criticism, disagreement or a perceived slight. They take it all as a personal attack.

Love

Narcissists do not know how to love. You might say to me, "Wait, what are you talking about Doc?" I'll stand by what I said: *They do not know how to love.* They can love wholeheartedly, *just not in the way most of us understand as love.*

Narcissists only know how to love to satisfy their needs and squelch their insecurities. *They are capable of love and empathy as long as it makes them feel good or they receive something in return.* Narcissists generally have faced abuse or trauma in childhood where they did not receive the love, respect or affection they craved. Leaving behind this huge gaping hole in their heart, which they constantly try to fill. Since they desperately seek love, appreciation, and constant affirmation to fill this hole they will automatically gravitate toward others who are sympathetic and can meet this impossible need.

It's an impossible task to fill the hole in anyone's heart, because as humans we can only fill our own void.

Eventually the narcissist will test and drain their partner with their outlandish criticism and pompous demands. Their insecurity gets heightened to the point of public humiliation. This is also the point where you are manipulated to alienate yourself from your friends and family. You become completely closeted with your narcissistic partner. The relationship becomes even more toxic.

The Narcissist

A narcissist is a person who is self-absorbed and who needs to exaggerate their own sense of importance. They must be in the spotlight wherever they go. They are the life of the party... we can say. That person who walks into a room and everyone stops talking because they are drawn to their energy. This is what feeds a narcissist's ego. They thrive on this attention and it's how a narcissist survives in the world.

Narcissists are extremely arrogant people and they don't have much empathy. They cannot understand someone else's pain, nor do they really care to. *They can't understand or feel anything that they have never personally experienced and they definitely can't understand the pain they put their partners through.* In fact, they believe you deserve all the pain that you are in. *"It's always your fault" "You brought this upon yourself."*

A narcissist is stuck somewhere between the ages of three to five years old where they are severely, emotionally stunted and underdeveloped. Despite how intelligent or socially high functioning they are, they have the emotional intelligence of an angry, irrational child. This is the reason they are so easily triggered by the slightest criticism and why they must always be right.

You see, the narcissist has unsuccessfully tried to detach and sever themselves from their inner demons, pains, and self-loathing from their childhood. It still exists and without taking ownership or embracing the hurts, the narcissist will not heal or evolve.

The emotional trauma will still linger on the surface where the narcissist will have underlying feelings of 'I am not good enough. I don't belong. People don't accept who I am. They cannot be trusted. They will hurt me if I don't get one up over them or hurt them first.'

The damage is so severe that there isn't a healthy self-identity that exists. Instead a false sense takes over which constantly needs to be fed. They must find ways to supply their ego with the validation that it needs. This is called 'narcissistic supply' also known as supplying the ego.

Since the narcissist does not take responsibility to heal from their trauma, they unconsciously project their self-hatred and loathing onto their partner, where they are convinced that they are the victim and their partner is the one who has the pathological behavior.

The wrath of anger they direct towards their partner is actually a reflection of how much they loathe themselves. For the narcissist, it's all about attacking to prevent becoming vulnerable. This allows them to gain control, which in turn feeds their egotistical narcissistic supply.

They are constantly covering up an insecurity that on a conscious level, they don't even know exists. The worst part is that they don't even have that concept.

There's no personal development ability. If they called you stupid, the rationale is that 'you made them call you stupid.' "I called you stupid because what you did was not smart." In other words, it's your fault if they called you stupid. The thought in their head is 'why don't you fix yourself and make yourself smarter so we can prevent this from happening again.'

The delivery is very logical and charming. It goes something like, "Sweetheart, you know what? I'm so sorry you were stupid. It's not my fault. Try to understand. It pains me that you act this way and that's why I must respond in kind. If you didn't do that (whatever you did), I wouldn't be calling you stupid. I'm trying to help you be a better person"

You begin to believe that you are stupid because you see the urgency in their eyes. This is complete brainwashing. Some people think this is an excuse the narcissist makes to be mean.

No, they 100% believe that you are stupid. The narcissist truly believes this from the core of their heart.

"I called you stupid because you are." *They think of themselves as the victim of your stupidity.* They base their opinion on what they feel is solid rationale, a no brainer. You are stupid. End of story.

That is their reality.

Exaggerated Self-Achievement & Status

Wherever a narcissist goes people are drawn to them. When they walk into a room, they are very charming... and they can sweep you right off your feet. They have the jokes you want to hear, and they know exactly how to get your attention.

When it comes to mental health, there's a whole class of delusional disorders. The narcissist is the king of 'Delusion of Grandeur.' For example, they believe they are the CEO and on top of that they believe they are on the Forbes list. They tell people, "I'm the CEO and I made this company what it is today." When in fact they might be out of a job. In other words, they tend to falsify their status.

Arrogance

The narcissist will walk around with a false sense of arrogance with nothing to show for it. They may not be educated or have money in the bank and yet give the impression of importance. Even if they are at the bottom of the bottom, they will walk around as if they own the world.

The narcissist engages in interpersonal exploitation to meet their own needs at the expense of the rights of others.

If they are a finance person they'd say, "I'm the top of the line, best in the stock market industry. I'm amazing. Everybody comes to me, I know everything. I know this, I know that. However, if you mention that you've heard that so-and-so is really good in this aspect you might get a response like: "What, him? You should try speaking with Charlie. He will validate that it's not true." Meanwhile, Charlie might not even exist, and who is even going to call Charlie to confirm?

The narcissist uses manipulation, lying, and anything else that will get them to the top of the game because they believe they are a supreme being.

There Are No Boundaries

They will cross every boundary you set and tear you apart to get whatever they need for themselves. This is done by disrespecting you with manipulation, even to the point of showing up at your door without permission. The narcissist might make up a story or even a huge lie about you, your friends or family... just to get what they want. They know how to press your buttons to manipulate you.

Behavior of the Narcissist

- They will blame and bully anyone attempting to hold them accountable.

- They circumvent accountability by attacking or accusing you.

- They argue until you are not only exhausted, you are confused. Very confused.

- They will deny the truth and rewrite the story. Hence your confusion.

- They will attempt to incite you in order to draw attention to you and away from them.

- They have the ability to take your small fear and turn it into paranoia.

- They will weave a dreadful outcome into a believable story. Hence your new paranoia.

Trauma Bonding

All the toxicity from the hurts and pains living with a narcissist becomes an addiction. Like the way Stockholm Syndrome presents: *The abused victim bonds with the abuser* since both are the source of terror and comfort to each other. *Anything is done by both parties to keep the relationship going.* As a result, the abused victim begins a strange unshakeable sense of loyalty and devotion to their abuser. Something most people from the outside just can't comprehend.

An abusive relationship is an addiction. It's a proven brain chemical imbalance. You get addicted to the Dopamine-Oxytocin-Serotonin cocktail your brain produces that comes from the highs of love bombing. You get the highs and then you get the lows and you're waiting for the highs again. It's tough.

When you remove yourself from the relationship, you go through withdrawal. This also happens when your narcissistic partner removes themself (ghosting) from the relationship. They have the ability to reach into your core so it's heavy work, but it can be done. It will be done.

Mind Fucking/Gaslighting

Intentionally making someone think they are wrong, even though they are right. This is called gaslighting. Narcissists gaslight others on a level that makes absolutely no sense and could be outright absurd. This behavior can include questioning your logical thoughts, making you doubt your perceptions or outright denying the reality of your experience.

Signs of Gaslighting

- They consistently disagree with details… that doesn't mean they are right.
- They question your facts, even more so in the face of evidence against them.
- They tell you that you don't see the world the right way – that their view is a more accurate version of the truth.
- They say they don't trust your perception because you've been wrong before.
- They invalidate what you say when it keeps them from getting their way.
- They fabricate complete stories convincing you that they are true.

Characteristic Phrases Thrown Out by Your 'Gaslighter'

- You don't know what you're talking about!
- You can't take a joke.
- You're crazy!
- You are just too sensitive.
- That wouldn't hurt my feelings.
- I'M NOT RAISING MY VOICE! *(while yelling at you)*

Victim Questions Reality

No. You are not losing your mind, you are experiencing gas-lighting as your narcissist plants seeds of doubt in your head in hopes that you begin to question your own memory, perception, and sanity... and you do.

When You Start Pulling Away

In a narcissistic relationship during the devaluation stage they can ghost you. When you start to defend yourself in an argument, your narcissist will threaten to leave you or just leave. If you follow them out to their car, they will ignore you.

You are so traumatically involved in the abuse that you may act out of character and attempt to even jump on top of their car, desperate to stop them from leaving. They will continue to ignore you and speed off, throwing you off the car and onto the street. You scream and they're gone. *In their head, they can't figure out why you are making a scene where they have to take such drastic measures to make them drive off on you.* There is no understanding on their part that you were desperate and hurt because they were abandoning you. No sadness. No remorse. It's simply not their fault. All they understand is that you made them do it.

Forgiveness

When the narcissist senses that you are starting to pull away, they will start asking for forgiveness to draw you back in. They might say, "I'm so sorry. Don't break us apart. You know I love you. The reason I'm doing this is because I had a bad childhood, but you're teaching me things. I see the beauty in our relationship."

Flying Monkeys

These are the narcissist's enablers. A narcissist will use their charms to convince and brainwash your friends and family to go against you. The narcissist makes sure that they are always portrayed as the victim. Any story they make up includes you as the villain. This is another way to control, manipulate, and isolate you.

Triangulation

When a narcissist feels that you are starting to pull away, they bring a third person into your relationship, this is called triangulation. The narcissist uses this person to instill feelings of jealousy and insecurity in you... their partner. This person is brought in to specifically control, dominate, and hurt you...the victim. It is the last resort when a narcissist realizes you have caught onto their game.

The Narcissist & The Codependent

The codependent and narcissist had a childhood of feeling rejected, unloved, abandoned, and unwanted. Both have internalized this abandonment into the very depths of their core where they carry it as an expression of shame. The codependent eventually figured out that by people-pleasing and prioritizing others' needs over their own, they are able to avoid either additional abandonment or criticism. While the narcissist did not find a solution or reprieve to avoid being rejected and hurt. Narcissists learned that the world can be a cold and harmful place. They understood it's better to punish than to be punished first.

Therefore, no matter how hard you try to love someone with a narcissistic personality disorder, they will never be able to return that love because *love, honesty, and vulnerability are viewed as threats to their survival* and they won't allow anyone to crawl under their skin to make them vulnerable.

The codependent always wants to fix a person and generally gravitates towards the wounded, since they don't believe the healthy would ever want them. By fixing the person they feel they are needed and in turn translates that need as love. Codependents never believe they alone could be enough. This is why when a narcissist gets upset with the codependent, not only will the codependent stay in the relationship, but they will do everything in their power to avoid displeasing the narcissist.

Codependency Dance

In the codependency narcissist dance, the two partners develop complementary roles to fill each other's needs. *The narcissistic person has found someone who puts their needs first and the codependent person has found a partner they can pour themselves into.* The narcissist has control over the codependent, which feeds their ego, while the codependent allows it because they interpret the control as love in their brain.

As the codependent, you get into a mental obsession where you don't want to lose your partner, this is due to the chronic narcissistic abuse cycle which initiates the trauma bond.

Empaths & Narcissists

Empaths are highly sensitive people who uniquely can sense or feel the emotions of people surrounding them. They are very intuitive and have high emotional intelligence. They are nurturing, very loving, and caring. They constantly want to fix and help, which makes them feel good about themselves. It gives them the security they seek. This is the perfect victim for a narcissist, because they thrive from the love and attention that they receive in order to fill their inner void.

The empath, after getting to know the narcissist, can feel their disturbances and pains. When they can feel something broken, they go into *savior mode* and try to fix their narcissist. A challenge that an empath can never win.

Narcissist: "Oh yes, please give me all of your love and attention. Wait, am I falling in love with you? I'm starting to feel vulnerable so I'm going to attack you before you can hurt me." (AKA: I can't let you control me. I must control you.)

Codependent Empath: "I'm going to shower you with so much love that you will be pleased with me. You will then understand how valuable I am and stay with me."
(AKA: I have a need to be loved, please fulfill it. I will control you with enough love that you won't hurt me.)

Cycle of Narcissistic Abuse

1. **Idealization also known as Love Bombing**
   This is the first phase of the cycle where the narcissist will do anything to sweep you off your feet. You are pursued, idealized, given gifts, and put on a pedestal. A fairytale being played out right before your eyes. You are told that you are sheer perfection. You are bathed in flattery and being set up for entrapment. Most importantly it can look like love, but it is not love... *it is obsession*. It is the phase that you cling onto when things start going downhill.

   Common Acts of Idealization by the Narcissist

   - Claims you have everything in common
   - Starts to plan your future together (within two weeks of the relationship)

- Compliments/admires everything about you
- Molds themself into everything you dream for in a partner
- Declares that you are their soulmate

2. **Devaluation Phase**

This phase overlaps somewhere in between the first phase of idealization. It usually starts when the narcissist is coming off the *high* of the love bombing. (AKA: The honeymoon period is over. The narcissist is getting bored. Fears and inner wounds begin to surface. It's time to feed their narcissistic supply and they start degrading you.)

Common Acts of Devaluation by the Narcissist

- Couldn't care less or be bothered if you are in trouble or in any threatening situation
- Unavailable when you are sick or need support of any kind
- "Tit for tat" will step on you further to prove a point.
- Verbal insults, gas-lighting
- Threatens abandonment
- Withholds information or sex
- Accusations

3. **Displacement**

This phase occurs when you provoke the narcissist's wrath by simply defending yourself. This is the last phase of the cycle, and it doesn't necessarily mean the end of the relationship. It means the narcissist now has made you their enemy and has set out to tear your life apart, which in turn fuels their narcissistic supply.

If the narcissist does understand that abandonment is what truly hurts you deeply, they will simply walk away. Knowing that you are in tremendous pain will also fuel their narcissistic supply which gives them satisfaction.

Commitment & The Narcissist

The narcissist doesn't understand commitment, yet they expect you to stay fully committed to them: their time, their ideas, and their life. They will show signs of commitment only when they want things in return, otherwise they do not follow through with their promises. They expect commitment from you, and they stay committed to their own routines and schedules.

Am I a Victim?

People aren't aware of the degrading and dehumanizing effects that the cycle of narcissism casts upon its targets.

People also aren't aware that it's even occurring to them.

You were idolized and then shoved off the pedestal in a slow, *put the frog in cold water and slowly turn up the heat* style.

The worst part is that you didn't even know how you became *a frog* from *a princess* in the first place.

Your sense of self was eroded. Perhaps you were even replaced and discarded multiple times, only to be lured back into the abuse cycle... one that was even more tortuous than before.

Maybe you were relentlessly stalked, harassed, and bullied to stay with your abuser.

Your entire reality has been warped and distorted. Yet there may not be visible scars to tell the tale; all you have are fractured memories and internal battle wounds. You may have placed your goals, hobbies, friendships, and personal safety on the back burner... just to ensure that your abuser felt *satisfied* in the relationship.

A lot of people think that mental abuse or any toxic relationship occurs in low socioeconomic environments or amongst uneducated people. That's why most people are surprised to know that many male narcissists generally target well educated, extremely smart, and very financially independent women. They are attracted to the confidence of these women.

The game of reeling them in validates the narcissist. 'I've got the CEO under my foot, groveling for me so I have to be amazing.' This is one of the thought processes that feeds their ego. It's like gasoline for a car, it's what fuels them.

Most of their victims have codependent personalities and are love deprived. So with the love bombing, their mindset is 'finally I'm getting the love that I deserve, this is what I've been looking for all of my life. This is my prince-charming.' What they don't realize is that this is not the *prince charming* that Disney was talking about.

The cycle of narcissistic abuse starts with the love bombing and then they start to devalue you ever so slowly. They might walk into the kitchen and observe you grabbing a cup for them. The first thing out of their mouth might be, "Oh honey, that's not how to hold a cup. You know you have to grab it from the bottom, not from the top. Who taught you this? Who would ever want to drink from that cup after you held it that way? Is this the etiquette that your parents taught you? Let me teach you how you really should hold a cup. It's so sad that your family didn't teach you right. I'm glad that I'm able to better you sweetheart."

Now the next time you are seen grabbing a cup *wrong* you get taunted, "Didn't I teach you the right way to hold a cup? What's wrong with you? I'm helping you, and you don't see it? Are you stupid?"

All of this went into your subconscious mind, where you now believe that your upbringing was terrible. Your family and you are low class and uncultured. You yourself didn't even notice the wrong, which makes you feel stupid. You question yourself for not having any manners and believe that something must be wrong with you. You now look at your knight in shining armor as superior as well as your savior since he is teaching you the right way to do things.

Eventually every time you go grab a cup, there will be a reminder of being reprimanded for holding the cup wrong.

That's just one cup incident.

You are constantly trying to please him to keep him from getting upset. You're always on your toes to do nothing wrong out of fear of losing the honeymoon phase of your relationship. As time progresses, every thought and action you do is preempted by 'what's the right way? or will this get him angry?' This is called *walking on eggshells*.

You go into severe anxiety and constantly feel on edge. You think twice about everything you do. It's mentally exhausting.

Meanwhile, you just want to go back to the love bombing stage of the cycle. You are addicted to that knight in shining armor... the charm, the flowers, and the truffles. You want that heavenly honeymoon again. You felt so good and happy.

When you're not in that phase, that's when you get the anxiety. That's how you go into depression. You get sad, you feel like you're not good enough. Nothing you do makes your narcissist happy. You feel like it's all your fault that things have gone bad.

At one point, something just clicks where you know this relationship does not serve you and you begin to pull back.

GET OUT - NO CONTACT

As I mentioned earlier there is a whole cycle to narcissistic abuse. The bond that you have between you and your narcissist is very strong because they know you so well that they can reach into your soul. There definitely is an energetic connection.

People tend to believe that everyone has only one soulmate. That person who is just for you for the rest of your life. This isn't true. A soulmate connection can be found in many forms with other people.

I know you don't want to hear that.

I do understand that the strong bond between you and your partner is real. There's also a difference between a healthy relationship and an unhealthy one. This is where the decision making comes in.

Once you've made the decision to live your life again, it will take discipline because your narcissist will attempt to contact you to draw you back into the relationship. Going No Contact will be one of the hardest things you will do.

NO CONTACT

Narcissists are very good in their capabilities of manipulating you... so you feel guilty; they *dupe* you into feeling bad to get you back into the relationship. They will even act like they regret all their past actions, as if they had some sort of an epiphany which then lures you back in.

Maybe you will go back because you deeply long for them. Perhaps the intense trauma and fear of loneliness is too difficult to bear. You can't seem to stop yourself from caving and making contact once again.

First and foremost, it is important that you understand that THIS IS NOT YOUR FAULT.

It is completely human for most people to break No Contact *repeatedly* because of the deep emotional level of trauma that they are in with their narcissist.

What No Contact means is that you made a mental decision that you are done. You have come to an understanding that this will not get better and there is no point to try anymore. You have exhausted all your resources to change this relationship into the potential you believe it could be.

Most importantly I would like to emphasize that No Contact = Self-Love: I love myself enough to get my life back from this soul slaughtering torture, and live *the love filled life* that I crave and deserve.

No Contact is Emotional as well as Physical

Being in No Contact doesn't just mean physically removing the narcissist out of your life. It also means to remove them emotionally. There are people who have been in No Contact for years and the narcissist still lives inside them as if the trauma and drama is still happening. The contact is still happening *in their very being*.

This is called Survival Recovery. This means, I'm physically out of the relationship but I have all the aftermath and unresolved issues still present. This is because I did not work on healing the holes that are in my consciousness that the narcissist had targeted in the first place.

When you are in Survival Recovery mode, you will do No Contact like a drug addict.

You might be obsessively checking their Facebook or any social channels that connect you to them, including their friends and family. You may look at old pictures or read through old texts and emails that you didn't delete. You might still have trinkets or gifts the narcissist bought you that bring back memories of better times.

If you do any of this... you are still in emotional contact. It is important for you to understand this *will* stunt your recovery.

This all needs to stop and be put away or thrown out. You must let go of the old to make room for the new. It is the law of attraction and healing.

The problem in today's millennia of the narcissistic realm is that we are making it all about the narcissist instead of healing ourselves.

"The *Narcissist did this...*"

"*The Narcissist did that...*"

"*Kill the Narcissist!*"

"*I must watch out for the next move the narcissist will make.*"

Don't get me wrong, it's all clearly understandable since they did completely torture you to the point where you felt as if they had ripped your soul apart.

No Contact Means It's All About YOU - Not Them

You did enough of the *focusing on the Narcissist*. You did it back then because you vehemently felt that you couldn't possibly live or breathe without them. Now you've made the decision to live for yourself. *You can and will live without them.*

This is the time to focus on healing your inner being and become your own source of love, approval, and security. Clearly you can understand now that *your narcissist can never fill any void for you*. It's time to fill your own void... to connect to your true power and higher consciousness, where you will feel indifferent to your ex-narcissist's existence.

A Narcissist will only belong where you keep them.

Rules of NO CONTACT:

Block and Delete them from Phones, E-mails, and all Social Media.

There is absolutely no need for you whatsoever to have an open line of communication between you and your narcissistic ex. You do not need to know what they are doing or be concerned if they are trying to get in touch with you or not. You do not need to check up on them.

Going No Contact does not mean it's ok for you to invisibly stalk them on social media and obsess over their possible new love interest. You are only hurting yourself, reinforcing your trauma, and delaying your healing process.

There will be times that you will wonder if they miss you or if they are trying to reach out to you. Part of your healing process is to release these thoughts and emotions so that you are not too bogged down by them.

Discipline yourself to give yourself the best life you deserve.
Block all the narcissistic person's possible social media
accounts. As well as those who are closely connected to them.
Do not answer any random texts that you don't know who
they are from and refuse to pick up any unlisted and
anonymous phone calls.

Remove all Friends, Family, and Pets associated with
the narcissist.

Free yourself from them. It will empower you. It is hurtful
and traumatic to leave friends that might have been in the
same circle as your ex-narcissist. It may be the only circle
you have or you have known them for years. It might be the
narcissist's children or pets and you felt very close to them.
Now you must leave them behind. There cannot be any
staying connected by proxy.

The Narcissist is known to manipulate others against their
partners. Abuse by proxy is very common, remember the
Flying Monkeys? You already went through horrific
heartbreak and torture. Now it's time to move on.

You'll have a healing shift once you get a clear understanding
that the Flying Monkeys, who have hurt you, are also in the
same boat as you were.

You see... just like you... the Flying Monkeys fall for the
narcissist's charm and get duped into believing the
narcissists *fabricated, victim suffering tale* that makes you
the devil incarnate.

Remember that when in public, the narcissist is always on
their best behavior with an outlandish display of affection
and love towards you so that the Flying Monkeys are
convinced that you *are* the problem. It's not too different in
the way your charming narcissist gas-lit you to believe that
you *were* really the problem. Understand that they were

being their authentic self from what they believed in, just as you had done.

Being angry at them is just pointless. *Forgive them and forgive yourself. Let go so you can live the happy life you desire and deserve.*

Why Do We Break No Contact?

Going No Contact is not easy. I myself broke it so many times initially. It is very common. You have been in a constant cycle of addiction - abuse and hurt - then attempts to try to get the narcissist to fix the hurts - abuse and hurt escalates in intensity - desperate attempts to try and get the narcissist to fix the hurts - and so on.

This cycle is imprinted in your brain and gut. It is an addiction... and not just a mental or physical addiction... a chemical addiction as well. The tidal waves of hormones are what your body craves. You are now going to go through intense withdrawal.

Being in this type of addiction is gut wrenching. You just can't seem to get a grip on yourself. You feel hooked to your narcissistic relationship as if you have lost your mind. You just can't get a hold of the highly charged urges and panic as your mind conjures up excuses. This makes you either reach out to the narcissist or allow their advances. You might even sneak around like some sort of drug addict, lying to yourself and hiding the fact you are seeing them behind everyone's back. You would sell your soul to just get *one glimmer of hope* out of your narcissist, regardless of what you must go through to get it.

You logically know this does not serve you and you are emotionally disconnected.

This is why it's important to face your emotional demons. You will need to reprogram your mind for your inner healing to be complete and sustainable.

The real truth about No Contact, without working on yourself, it is exhausting. Once you start working on your emotional healing and do your inner work, you will not bite when the narcissist tries to approach you or aggravate you with their usual attention seeking habits. You just won't care and will find them easy to ignore. You will come to the clear understanding that your life has absolutely nothing to do with your ex-narcissist. Initially No Contact can be stressful. Imagine doing it with children. It's not easy.

Co-Parenting with a Narcissist

Co-parenting means two parents who work as a team in the upbringing and caregiving of their child, with mutual goals of providing the best possible healthy environment.

This is NOT possible with a narcissist.

A narcissist will disagree with anything you suggest. They can refuse to stick to prior arrangements or just not show up to pick up the children. They will interfere with the child's schedule and appointments. They'll keep you in ongoing court and custody battles.

In true form, the narcissist will use the children as weapons to trigger you. They will do anything to not cooperate with you. This is how the narcissist continues their abuse and control. As a parent, you will worry about how your children are being treated. You'll be concerned if they are witnessing too much conflict between the two of you or if the narcissist is turning your kids against you. You may even be worried that they are turning your child into a narcissist.

Talking or lecturing your ex-narcissist on the importance of maintaining a healthy relationship for the kids will not bring you any positive results. It will only help to add fuel to their narcissistic supply allowing them to act up further against you. This is where Parallel Parenting comes into play.

Parallel Parenting - Modified No Contact

You can't completely go No Contact when you share children with a narcissist. It must be modified for the best interest of you and your children. Some call this Modified No Contact.

Parallel Parenting is an arrangement where the parents are disengaged from each other and have limited direct contact. This will automatically enforce boundaries and take away the power from the narcissist.

Rules of Modified Contact - In Addition to No Contact

The best thing you can do is to have a strict parenting plan in place. This is called a Parenting Agreement, which is a legal parenting plan.

Make a Parenting Plan

It must be detail oriented where there are no grey areas and incorporates complete elimination of contact between each other.

This would mean...

- No children's birthday parties together.

- You each have specific designated times for school and sporting events.
- There is no contact for drop off and pick up
- The parents can pick up from school directly and drop back off to school or arrange a third party for the exchange of children.
- The ex-narcissist cannot just show up at your home
- There are now third-party phone applications. available for co-parenting communication. This portal is the only way you and the narcissist communicate. All communication is recorded and cannot be erased. It is admissible in court.
- Stick to your parenting agreement, I'll say that again... STICK TO YOUR PARENTING AGREEMENT.

Victim Energy

Always remember that children are resilient, and it is important to work on your emotional healing to come out of the victim energy you are in. Victim energy can be very toxic which will lead you into not having the ability to give your children the attention they require.

Parental Alienation

How can you give any attention to your children when your narcissistic ex is constantly looking for every opportunity to trigger you? It takes a great deal of neural energy to process our emotions.

One of the most common tactics and issues victims of narcissistic abuse face is Parental Alienation. This is when the narcissistic parent manipulates a child to dislike the other parent. This could lead to the child rejecting you. In this situation, it's most important not to retaliate and not bad mouth the other parent to them.

Take a step back and empower your children with your own healing shift. Lead by example. Children can see and understand how you are and the role you've taken in your life towards peace and happiness. They will feel your new-found energy and that power alone will have your child gravitate towards you and your new beautiful life together.

No Contact

1. Awareness of the capabilities of a narcissist
2. Acceptance that you are in a toxic relationship
3. Understand why the relationship does not serve you
4. Decision and discipline of letting go
5. No contact (even with shared custody of children)

Grey Rock Method

In today's world, I have read and heard many people suggest that when you are in a narcissistic relationship the best way to avoid confrontation or to make a narcissist lose interest in you is to act like a Grey Rock. It is the methodology of limited contact, rather than going No Contact. If you are being told to Grey Rock, this means to completely detach from your emotions and feelings... to become as dull, boring, and lifeless as a grey rock when dealing with a narcissist. In other words, to become invisible. This way the narcissist will lose interest in you and seek for their supply elsewhere.

I find this methodology hurtful for the victim and I do not advocate it. The issue is *never* about the narcissist. The issue is how much power you choose to give away in caring about their actions. I am more interested in empowering my clients to respect and assert their own boundaries.

The fact that you are consciously executing this act of *being dull and emotionally disconnected* means that you are still feeding the narcissist. You are not protecting yourself and you are validating their behavior. That's not healing. In fact, that's exhausting. It's also mentally depressing not to be your true self.

Actual disconnection with a narcissist is not a self-disciplined, logical or physical act. It is a deep inner healing that must take place where disconnect comes naturally. The Grey Rock Method will not help the hurts, pains, and obsessive thoughts that still linger inside your head. In fact, you are actually causing more trauma to yourself and digging an even deeper hole. With Grey Rocking, you are intentionally losing your connection to your own needs, feelings, and wants where you risk becoming alienated from your true self just to avoid the narcissists' antics.

This approach requires you to suppress your natural need for love, attention, and affection. The behavior of becoming invisible supports the belief of self-sacrifice and self-denial in order to obtain happiness. This feeds further codependency, making those deep chords of codependent trauma even thicker. The thicker the cord, the more difficult to cut.

Grey Rocking can also draw further abuse from the narcissist, since suddenly the narcissistic supply has been stopped, by you acting indifferent. They will find new and even more intense ways to abuse you. Remember, the narcissist is goal driven to get their control back.

If there are children involved the narcissist will use them to provoke a response, making it easy for you to cave from Grey Rocking. There are no limits for a narcissist's behavior. They need the satisfaction of knowing that their victim still has feelings for them. If your narcissist has a physical, violent nature then you may be taking a chance in putting yourself in harm's way.

Subconscious Use of Grey Rocking

If the victim is not healed, they may even subconsciously use this methodology as a weapon to get back at the narcissist and/or have a self-sabotaging behavior of hope that this action of indifference may elicit a miraculous realization for the narcissist to change.

I believe the Grey Rock method causes more damage than sustainable healing. When you're healed from within, you don't care anymore what circus act the narcissist may play in front of you. It won't even phase you as the narcissist is just not an entity in your life anymore, because of your healing journey within. You grew way past them. In fact, you would most probably grab some popcorn, pull up a chair, and watch the show instead.

Chronic Abuse & Flashbacks

A victim of chronic abuse usually ends up dealing with severe anxiety, depression, emotional flashbacks, and complex post-traumatic stress disorder.

When it comes to flashbacks, a victim's mind goes to all sorts of abusive incidents from the past. For example, if your narcissist had always given you a hug and said, "I'm sorry" after the abuse, then watching them hug your child might create a flashback. It might remind you how easy it was for them to hurt you and then hug you.

Even if you see them smile in a certain quirky way again, you will associate it with how they used to do that after they had severely tortured you. Therefore, it's important to work on your emotional healing, on your way to full recovery.

The Effects of Narcissistic Abuse on the Recipient

Mental	• Questions Own Sanity • Loss of Confidence • Self Esteem in Tatters
Physical	• Fear of Safety • Exhausted/Loss of Energy • Decline in Health, ex. Adrenal Fatigue as most common
Psychological	• Living in Fear • Anxiety • Depression • PTSD/CPTSD
Social	• Loss of Reputation • Loss of Social Network • Loss of Family, Friendships, Relationships • Isolation
Sexual	• Loss of Pleasure • Trust • Loss of Self-Worth
Spiritual	• Lose Your Inner Being/Soul/Spirit • Question Own Spiritual Beliefs, i.e. God/Universe

MY SOULMATE MY LOVE MY NARCISSIST

The Narcissist's Prayer

That didn't happen.

And if it did, it wasn't that bad.

And if it was, that's not a big deal.

And if it is, that's not my fault.

And if it was, I didn't mean it.

And if I did...

You deserved it.

-Unknown

MOVING FORWARD

Those of us who have experienced narcissistic abuse will be required to heal in order to live life again. The good news is that healing is possible. We do need psychotherapy and yet conventional healing is only the first step. There might be a need for medication just to help re-regulate the nervous system, reduce anxiety, and lift depression. Knowing why you are using medication is what's important.

Medication doesn't resolve what's really going on in your brain. It doesn't take away the pain. Typically, psycho-pharmaceuticals just alleviate symptoms. Like a bandage, they have an almost masking effect and do not heal you. Many will wish for or even desperately seek a quick pill to just get rid of the debilitating pain. They want to numb out. I wish it were that easy.

The biological piece of abuse comes from being addicted to the narcissistic cycle of abuse. The Dopamine, endogenous opioids, and all the different hormones that get produced flood your brain and that's how you get into trauma bonding. When you remove yourself, you will go into withdrawal. Remember, an abusive relationship is an addiction.

Adrenal Fatigue

It is astonishing how much emotional health can influence a person's physical health.

Adrenal Fatigue can be considered a mind-body disorder. A strong mind-body connection is a powerful healing force you can harness for better health. However, on the flip side in Adrenal Fatigue the mind-body connection can be a devastatingly negative force capable of ruining your body.

If you have constitutionally weak adrenal glands at birth, stress may cause this weakness to be expressed leading to Adrenal Fatigue. The absence of stress on the other hand, can delay the expression of this weakness for an indefinite period of time. As you age your genes do not change, however your epigenome can change dramatically. It is influenced by the physical and emotional stressors you expose yourself to and how you respond to those stressors within your environment. This is what ultimately affects your epigenome.

A narcissistic abusive relationship can influence the expression of your genes, and directly impact your tendency to avoid or develop many unpleasant conditions from heart palpitations and Adrenal Fatigue to depression. The ability to have a positive mental attitude greatly affects your physical health. This is true in the case of Adrenal Fatigue. In fact, if emotional stressors are present and not resolved, they can act as a deterrent to Adrenal Fatigue recovery.

Correcting Adrenal Fatigue often causes a person to begin to live at a much deeper level and to understand the body and mind from a more spiritual perspective as well. It forces us to focus on what is truly important in life-such as peace, love, forgiveness, contentment.

The healing of the mind must occur before healing of the physical body... because the mind controls the body. Our healing process begins with the removal of emotional baggage from abusive relationships.

Unless you remove the toxic relationship from your life, the constant negative energy flow needed to sustain the toxicity prevents Adrenal Fatigue healing. Channeling the toxic negative energy into positive constructive energy is the key to the Quantum healing process of the mind, body, and spirit.

Post-Traumatic Stress Disorder (PTSD) & Complex Post Traumatic Stress Disorder (C-PTSD) are common in women who have been victims of narcissistic abuse. They almost always leave the relationship with PTSD or C-PTSD.

Post-traumatic stress results from experiencing a devastatingly stressful event or series of events in a short period of time. There is a perceived sense of helplessness and one's sense of self is annihilated. According to the American Psychiatric Association, PTSD is a mental disorder that can develop after a person is exposed to a traumatic event such a sexual assault, warfare, traffic collisions or other threats on a person's life.

Symptoms may include disturbing thoughts, feelings or dreams related to an event or events. These symptoms last for more than a month after the event has occurred.

C-PTSD is similar to PTSD, resulting from persistent and continuous psychological trauma for long periods of time. It is the chronic and repetitive trauma occurring that makes the victim believe there's no possibility of escape. There is a perceived sense of helplessness and *one's sense of self is annihilated.*

In a narcissistic abusive relationship when the *victim* tries to leave... the narcissist retaliates by stalking, harassing, and intimidating their partner until they come back. This causes the partner to feel hopelessly trapped with the impossibility to escape, thus experiencing C-PTSD. For example, if the narcissist physically assaulted their partner or someone their partner loves... this can result in PTSD; the loved one may even be a pet.

When it comes to PTSD, intentional shocks inflicted by humans are the most difficult to heal from and these include sexual, physical, and emotional abuse. With regards to significance, these events fall directly under combat and resistance fighting such as those that occur in the military.

Individuals who have been in a relationship with a narcissist, might suffer from the following...

- Re-experiencing aggressive acts and comments made by the narcissist (can include bad dreams and nightmares).
- Hypersensitivity – trouble sleeping, being easily frightened, difficulty with concentrating, and outbursts of anger.
- Anxiety – being in constant fight-or-flight mode. This in turn leads to physical and emotional fatigue, which later manifest as illness and disease in the body.
- Being triggered by stimuli in the environment which recalls traumatic memories.
- Repetition Compulsion – Reenacting traumatic events in an attempt to gain closure – this is why we often re-abuse ourselves after our abuser has left. This might include stalking him or her online to see them with a new partner, negative self-talk or entering another abusive relationship. In other words, trying to complete what wasn't previously completed. However, this only enhances the symptoms of PTSD, because it doesn't heal the trauma.

If left untreated, PTSD and C-PTSD lead to other symptoms and conditions which affect all areas of life including...

- Inability to handle stress
- Eating disorders
- Drug and alcohol addictions
- Damaged relationships with others
- A negative outlook on life

- Depression
- Specific anxiety disorders such as panic attacks and phobias. For example, victims who were stalked often develop agoraphobia.
- Crippled Self-Esteem
- Loss of career and loss of desire to be productive
- Diseases such as cancer.
- Victims of abuse have a higher incidence of certain types of cancer.
- Suicide Ideation
- Suicide

Holistic Healing

Once you've made the decision to permanently remove yourself from your toxic relationship it's time to work on your own healing. This is what allows you to heal from the inside out. You must work on the inside before you can work on the outside. Holistic healing involves meditation, energy work, and reprogramming your mindset. That's where Quantum healing comes into play because it's about working with your innate intelligence patterns, the energy you hold in your body and within your subconscious beliefs.

Holistic healing brings sustainable core healing.

Then there's understanding perspectives of why this happened to you. How come you allowed these things? Why were you so enamored with the whole situation?

Real healing is about self-forgiveness and doing your own personal work. One of the best things you can do is to learn how to stop, take a breath, feel your emotions, and think before you speak. Finding your happy place within your mind... mine is in a garden...and counting the gifts you see, brings a deep sense of calm and gratitude into your life.

Take Deep Breaths

Shallow breaths are when we take in air and our chest rises. Belly breaths are considered deep breaths and bring more oxygen and calm to our nervous system. The easiest way to learn how to do a belly breath is to place a hand on your belly and open your mouth. As you breathe in through your mouth, your tummy looks and feels like a balloon being inflated. Once you take a breath, blow it out through pursed lips. In other words, put your lips in the position just before kissing someone. Another term would be fish lips.

Feel Your Emotions

Reacting comes from not wanting to feel our emotions. When someone says something, embrace it and avoid labeling what was said as good or bad. This gives you a moment to respond appropriately. When it comes to self-love and self-care, it saves you from triggering.

A trigger response is when something in the present reminds you of the past.

Smells are known to be the most common triggers. We might smell a cake and be transported back to a family birthday party. It might have been a really happy and joyful time. That same smell might transport us to a memory when a cake was being thrown at us as well. So, smell elicits both positive and negative memories.

We can avoid future triggers by acknowledging that something hurt or felt uncomfortable, right when it happens. At times, it's good to replace the smells with better and happier new memories. That way the same smell will now trigger you to a new happier and more positive memory.

Think Before You Speak

We can get in touch with our emotions even before we speak. This way we can respond appropriately and save ourselves a great deal of heartache. When we are upset, we react. After all we are human beings. It takes discipline to think before we react or speak. Taking a moment to connect with what just happened or what we were just told, allows us to connect with ourselves so we can appropriately connect with others. When we do acknowledge that something was hurtful, we can communicate that fact. Maybe not in the moment but later. We can let the other person know how they hurt us. This works well unless we are dealing with a narcissist.

When you feel and understand your emotions before you react, you are the one who is in control... it's very empowering. Triggers come from what has been said or done to us in the past. Understanding where a trigger is coming from helps us respond rather than react.

Check in with yourself before you respond. Take three deep breaths, not shallow ones. Really feel those breaths. Relax your abdomen as you breathe in and squeeze it as you breathe out.

Count the Gifts

Everyone has their own happy place, for me it's a garden. When I hear 'look around and count the gifts in your life' I'm transported to a garden. I see flowers, butterflies, and trees. I feel the sunlight on my face and smell the sweetness of the grass. I start thinking about how beautiful and miraculous the universe really is and then I begin to count my blessings.

Even though there is happiness all around us, we can get so stuck on what we define as happiness that we stop seeing what is already there. We can ground ourselves by looking around and receiving what we already have. In turn, this opens the door to possibility from a place of empowerment rather than lack. Smell the flowers, hear the birds, and walk barefoot on the grass or wade in the ocean. Find your happy place, the one you can easily go to in your mind.

When you go to your happy place, it triggers beautiful memories. These are the memories that make us feel warm, cared for and loved. This is when we can easily tap into the thoughtfulness of others. Counting your gifts goes beyond gratitude for having a house or a car.

There are many gifts that we can receive from others or even give to others: the gift of love, the gift of creativity, the gift of kindness, the gift of positivity, etc.

I have included information from my thesis as to how my clients have come about their healing and recovery through a *three-step process* using the Quantum Approach and its various modalities.

The *first step* is bringing forth insight of their relationship by *discerning* their *self* and understanding their relationship with the cycle they have been in. The *second step* is *renewal & reprogramming*, focusing on rebuilding the self and redefining relationships, and the *third step* is *transformation* in order to have new perspectives towards positive thinking, creativity, manifestation, and empowerment.

3 Step Process of Recovery & Healing
from an Abusive Relationship with a Narcissist

INSIGHT	RENEWAL & REPROGRAMMING	TRANSFORMATION
Discerning *The Self*	**Rebuilding** *The Self* **& Identity**	**New Prospective**
Self-Esteem *Self-Love* *Fear* *Anxiety*	*Forgiveness* *Empowerment*	*Positive Thinking* *Creativity* *Manifestation* *Affirmations*
Understanding Relationships & Cycle of Abuse	**Redefining Relationships**	
	Developing Boundaries *Assertiveness* *Codependency*	

INSIGHT

Discerning the Self

You can look back in the past and long for the person you once were before the narcissistic relationship. Today you are wiser. It's not about going back to the old you, it's about growing and blossoming yourself into the new you. The today you, where you are learning to heal and finding beauty in life once again. When you understand and accept that you are enough, you can conquer the world.

Self-Esteem

We are perfectly imperfect. Even with all of our flaws, we are amazing! It's much easier to love ourselves when we admit that we are doing the best that we can with the tools that we already have within us. When we really love ourselves, we can see how wonderful we are from the inside out. This is the way that we can understand that we are whole enough, and there is no void to fill. Now we love without expectation. The addictive pattern of pleasing so we can get something in return, no longer has a hold on us.

Self-Love

Love is like an overflowing cup. If you don't fill up your own cup first, you have nothing to give to yourself and others. I believe that as women, we tend to forget to fill up our cup. When we don't have the overflow, it's exhausting. Life becomes a plethora of frustration, anger, and sadness. It brings out every negative emotion in you because you are not happy.

If you are angry with yourself for being in a relationship with a narcissist, it's important for you to know and acknowledge that you believed in something. You were able to love with your whole heart, mind, and soul. *There's no point in being angry about being a good person.*

Your heart had the compassion to attempt to change someone and bring out the beauty in them. You believed in their potential and you did the best you could. You also learned that we can't change anyone.

Now you know that it's okay, and we can't *save* everyone. We all have our own walk and work to do. It's important to know that we don't complete each other, we complement each other. That's huge.

Fear

The fear of being abandoned, taken for granted, ignored as if we never existed stems from our own insecurities. When we do not feel complete within ourselves, we look for it in someone else. Your narcissist provides all that is needed and more until they get bored.

Facing the fear and understanding where it comes from allows us to accept the reality of our circumstances.

Anxiety

When we are anxious, we can feel our heartbeat. There are many physical signs of anxiety. For example, rapid heart palpitations and chest pains. It's a psychological state that is felt within the body.

Changing our perceptions and reframing our stories helps us to relieve and view anxiety in a different light.

Understanding the Relationship & Cycle of Abuse

The cycle of abuse often includes an abuser who craves control over their victim. If the victim does not please the abuser, the abuse will intensify. In some situations, such as narcissistic abuse, the abuser cannot see him or herself and does not understand that they are abusive. They believe their partner is making them act a certain way.

RENEWAL & REPROGRAMMING

Rebuilding *The Self* & Identity

Beauty is all around us. It's about making the time to actually see it and enjoy it. To begin with, its understanding that we are all connected in one way or another and that energy can be felt and recognized within us. Incorporating mindfulness and meditation into our daily routine, can significantly change our lives. Keep it simple. Mindfulness can be done even while washing dishes or taking a shower. Listening to the water running is a great way to step into a meditation. A salt lamp, essential oils or a burning candle really isn't necessary. It's definitely a nice addition and has great benefits yet it's really not necessary to connect with yourself.

Mindfulness and meditation are other forms of self-love and self-care.

I'm big on grounding myself, especially before going to bed. I keep a small packet of lavender on my nightstand. I smell it by taking a couple of deep breaths through my nose. It's very calming. When I close my eyes, I take all my day's worries and push them out with the exhale through my mouth.

You can also ground yourself in the morning, before you even get out of bed. I like to stretch out, close my eyes, and take 3 deep breaths. Starting from the top of my head... I visualize sunlight filled with abundance, love, peace, and happiness flowing through my body... creating a positive energy bubble around me.

Forgiveness

This concept and mind shift is for our own benefit and healing. Forgiveness isn't about getting closure with another person. It's about releasing the hold the other person has on us.

We often think of forgiveness as something to do for other people, it's done for us and sometimes we need to forgive ourselves as well.

Empowerment

Victimhood is the opposite of empowerment. When we are a victim, there is always someone else to blame. Stepping out of victimhood means learning *what is* and *what is not* our responsibility.

Being empowered to choose your emotions and rewrite your story puts you in charge of your life. This way the drama of victimhood ceases, the nervous system is calmer, and the adrenals have a chance to be restored.

Redefining Relationships

Society defines and teaches us that there is a right way or a wrong way to do relationships, whether it's being a girlfriend, fiancé or wife. We end up finding that it's not that simple. Society is *not* what dictates healthy relationships, we do. We get to define that for ourselves in any relationship. This also includes the relationships we have as a daughter, mother, and friend... not just the one with our partner.

Developing Boundaries

The narcissist does not value your No. Setting a boundary with your narcissist is like setting up a challenge. It is one of the hardest things to do. They are all over the place - all of the time - not just in person, also emotionally, spiritually, and psychologically. They do not care about other people's space and time. Their only concern is about *their own boundaries* and they protect *their own space* very well.

The moment you put your foot down you will experience threats, anger, and even rage. Toxic people will make you feel like you are holding a grudge against them, when you are really just holding your boundaries.

Assertiveness

Standing up for your beliefs is about respecting yourself. Assertiveness comes from developing self-love and exercising your rights calmly without aggression.

Speak up. What doesn't serve you, doesn't serve you. Being assertive around your boundaries is essential for inner peace.

Codependency

The worst part of codependency is doing everything in your power to avoid displeasing your narcissist. Now it's time to learn how to gravitate *away* from wounded people by becoming healthy yourself.

Learning that you are enough and believing that you *can* love yourself, alleviates your codependent need for love no matter what it may cost you. Pleasing yourself becomes your number one priority.

TRANSFORMATION

New Perspective

The energy from positive perspectives and positive thinking helps to heal us and move us forward. This is all part of Mind, Body, and Spirit healing.

Positive Thinking

Shifting the mind can easily be done with one-to-one discussions and energy work. The emotions we hold within, stay with us if we don't allow them to move through us.

Reprogramming the mind allows us to get clarity and perspective of the situation at hand. Creating a positive mindset is about breaking negative patterns from our past. Sometimes bitterness and unfulfilled expectations can cloud judgement.

Creativity

Getting creative is part of problem solving. When you are too tired to think, you can't be creative. If your life is lived from *do, do, do mode* you won't have enough space for creativity. Making decisions based on respecting yourself opens you up to new possibilities that allow you to step away from a life that does not serve you.

Manifestation

Being fully present, knowing what you want, letting go of the outcomes, and holding space for the impossible is what manifestation is all about. Knowing the *how* is not part of manifestation. The how will reveal itself during the manifestation process. To manifest means to see what is already there. Limiting beliefs and fatigue keep us from seeing other possibilities. They also hold us back from energetically pulling in what we truly desire.

Affirmations

We listened to our narcissistic partner because we believed they were helping us to be better; we also listened to them in order to please them, because we wanted something in return. We wanted love.

Once my clients realize the truth of each of the statements on the following page. I have them repeat a statement in front of the mirror.

When a client steps into an A-ha moment, I choose an appropriate affirmation...

- ❖ I love myself unconditionally.

- ❖ I am STRONG!

- ❖ I allow only healthy and loving relationships into my life.

- ❖ Life wants what is best for me. I am OK with where I am right now.

- ❖ I am connected and comfortable in all environments, with all people.

- ❖ I find and enjoy the simple pleasures life is offering right now.

- ❖ How I feel matters; I concentrate on aspects of life that make me feel good!

- ❖ My challenges bring me better opportunities.

- ❖ My mood creates a physiological response in my body.

- ❖ I am peaceful and positive.

- ❖ I am in control of my thoughts and my life.

- ❖ I love myself and who I am.

Establishing Stability

Conventional healing focuses on symptom relief and is often referred to as Allopathic Medicine. Holistic Medicine focuses on the cause of one's symptoms and the patterns that lead to those symptoms. *Quantum Medicine focuses on and shifts the energies that make up causes, patterns, and symptoms.*

Based on quantum physics and the power of consciousness, Quantum Medicine seeks to integrate various parts of conventional and alternative medicine.

The quantum entanglement of body, mind, and spirit was proven almost 100 years ago by Albert Einstein, Erwin Schrodinger, Werner Heisenberg, Niels Bohr, Wolfgang Pauli, and Fritz Popp. They proved the pre-eminence of energy over matter in the most successful theory of mathematics and physics in human history; this was known as the Copenhagen interpretation of quantum mechanics.

Epigenetics is part of quantum physics and works through chemical tags, added to chromosomes, that in effect switch genes on or off.

Understanding Epigenetics

Bruce Lipton changed my world in the way he explained Epigenetics. He has a sense of peace about everything. Dr. Lipton is amazing, and he's known as the Father of Epigenetics. His work and research are foundational to all that I do with my clients. When I find an understanding or method that really works, I stick with it and implement it in the work that I do.

"Conventional belief was that your life to a large degree was determined by your heredity. The new science of Epigenetics says, no, your life is a result of your participation and your mind's influence on what's going on." ~Bruce Lipton

Reprogramming your genes starts with reprogramming your mindset. Negativity can drastically impact our cells.

Our mind has control over our body and our healing. The more our mind reprograms into positivity and being limitless, the more we move away from limiting beliefs and start understanding our cultural biases. We begin to live in a healthier state of mind. This is called mind-body healing.

Your life is a result of the participation of your mind. Our mind can influence what's going on at a cellular level. The good news is that you can completely reconstruct your genes by turning certain genes on or off. This is what is meant by the statement *you can change your genes*.

Conscious & Subconscious

Neuroscience has recognized that the subconscious controls ninety-five percent of our lives. Since the subconscious programs operate outside the range of consciousness, we don't experience ourselves playing out these behaviors. Therefore, we don't even see ourselves sabotaging our own lives and as a result we don't take responsibility for the lives we lead.

We see ourselves as victims of forces outside of our control. It's hard to own what we've done our whole lives. So we perceive ourselves as victims and we believe that our genes are in control.

Recognizing and reprogramming our subconscious beliefs to remove limiting negative beliefs is part of *Quantum Based Transformational Life Coaching*. This helps create tools to rewrite destructive programs that occupy our subconscious field.

Modern research today is proving the validity of quantum healing in the fields of acupuncture, homeopathy, homotoxicology, and other energy-based traditions.

Perception

By changing your perception, your mind can alter the activity of your genes and create over thirty thousand variations. You can literally rewrite those genetic programs through changing your mindset, which in turn changes your blood chemistry.

Removing limiting beliefs and fears is also important. For example, if you were married to your narcissist, your thoughts might have sounded like this: *I don't want to be a divorcee. I don't want to be known as a divorcee, etc.* You may fear religious, societal, family or cultural backlash from going through with a divorce.

People might say, "Your family broke up." You can say, "No, this is my family. My kids and I 'are' my family."

EFT

Emotional Freedom Technique (EFT) is an energy psychology process where the individual taps energy meridian points, on the body, especially on the face. This is done to release negative emotions surrounding an incident or issue. EFT is based on the Thought Field Therapy techniques developed by Dr. Roger Callahan in California in the late 1980s where it is believed that all negative emotions are a result of an imbalance in the body energy system. Eastern traditions have been aware of the meridians of energy for thousands of years.

The meridian network was detailed in the first medical account of acupuncture in The Yellow Emperor's Classic of Internal Medicine, which dates from the Han Dynasty (206 BCE to 220 ACE). A simple way to describe EFT would be that it is like emotional acupuncture, without the needles.

An EFT is applied by tapping (teaching the client to tap as well) with the fingertips on certain meridian points, stimulating the blocked energy so that it starts flowing freely again. While tapping the client focuses on negative feelings, thoughts, and emotions as well as experiences.

For people who have gone through toxic narcissistic abuse resulting in anxiety, PTSD, and C-PTSD there are special EFT methods such as the Tearless Trauma Technique which allows them to recall any incident in a safe and pain-free environment. Sometimes relief can be experienced almost immediately.

The memory is not taken away, instead the negative emotions are neutralized so that the person does not have to relive the physical symptoms of the trauma over and over again, as if they were there. Through this mode of technique, healing takes place as the body and mind become calm and energetically balanced.

Reiki

The healing technique called Reiki was developed by the Japanese Buddhist Mikao Usui, in 1922. Reiki comes from the Japanese word (Rei) which means "universal life" and (Ki) which means energy.

Reiki is not affiliated with any particular religion or religious practice. It is not massage nor is it based on belief or suggestion. Reiki is a subtle and effective form of energy work using spiritually guided life force energy. It can either be *hands-on* where a Reiki practitioner will apply a light touch during the session or *hands-off* where they will hold their hands slightly above the body.

Life energy (Reiki) flows through all living things. Reiki practitioners understand that everyone has the capability to connect with their own healing energy and use it to strengthen energy in themselves and help others. It is believed that a person's Ki or energy should be strong and free flowing. When this is true, a person's body and mind is in a positive state of health. When the energy becomes weak or blocked it could lead to symptoms of physical or emotional imbalance.

Reiki eases the tension and stress that has built up from the cyclic abuse. It will help support the body to facilitate an environment for healing on all levels: physical, mental, and emotional.

The reason Reiki can be so powerful and effective is because it infuses your chakras and your body with the energy of the universe. Your body takes exactly what it needs at that point in time. The Reiki practitioner's role is to act as a channel of universal energy to help facilitate healing, so that the body can heal itself.

When you infuse Reiki into areas of the body that are energetically or physically weak, the healing process can begin as your body allows itself to fully release.

Chakras

It is now well established that the mind, in giving wrong meaning to an experience, can produce disease. (Dossey, 1992). Dr. Bruce Lipton, as mentioned earlier and who has done considerable research in Epigenetics, talks about how our minds can rewrite our genes. He compares a cell to a computer chip, as each holds a *bit* of information. Both can receive information through different routes and cause a reaction.

Even though the programming of the cells begins in infancy or before birth, they can be reprogrammed to act differently. The process which the information goes through to affect a cell, determines the programming of that cell.

Cells become cancerous because they are instructed in some way to do so. If we realize this and change our beliefs, thus changing our messages to our cells, we can heal ourselves.

A person who goes through a *heartbreak* might formulate a decision to avoid all future romantic love, due to its diversity. Eventually the prolonged inattention to the heart chakra, the chakra where romance is experienced, can bring about a heart correlated disease.

When the immune system goes awry, the body loses its ability to distinguish potential cancer cells and does not kill them off. This might lead to a malignant growth. It's crucial to keep your mind from giving the wrong meaning to situations.

In my experience, women who have undergone the abuse from narcissistic abusive relationships have strong blockage of the vital energy in their heart chakra. The blockage formulates from all the pain and distress they have gone through as well as stopping themselves from romantic love in the future out of the fear of pain, distress, and lack of trust.

Statistically it has been shown that women, who have undergone abusive relationships, have a higher rate for developing cancer than all other post ailments. In order to heal, she must take a quantum leap in her mind and rediscover the value of love. Only then can quantum healing occur. This is why meditation is a key factor for reprogramming thinking towards a positive state of mind.

The word chakra comes from an ancient Indian language known as Sanskrit. Chakra means vortex or spinning wheel. The chakras spin in a clockwise (inward) direction and look like a spinning fan.

Each chakra spins at its own frequency ensuring that the Ki (energy) is drawn into the body to keep the physical, mental, emotional, and spiritual health of the body in balance. The chakras also spin counterclockwise (outward) when releasing unwanted Ki (energy) or when they are dealing with other people or situations.

Chakras are *energy centers where energy enters and leaves our bodies.* They affect every part of our being. When we are feeling good, relaxed, and happy in the world our chakras are spinning evenly. This creates a balanced aura which keeps our body well protected. However if we are feeling depressed, anxious or stressed, then the chakras will be depleted, and our aura may also be affected. Over time this will negatively affect a person's well-being. *This is where Reiki would be very beneficial.* None of our chakras works independently of the other chakras. They constitute a whole energy system.

Chakras only work fully when the other chakras are fully engaged. Each chakra has a role in balancing some aspect of our life physically, emotionally, spiritually, and mentally.

The following information is a breakdown of each chakra and how to spot the imbalances that can manifest on emotional, spiritual, and physical levels.

The Seven Chakras for Healing
(7th chakra located above the head)

1st Chakra/*Root* Chakra - Basic Trust

This chakra is located between the genitals and the anus. The root chakra deals with the issues surrounding identity, survival, connection to earth, and tribal issues. When this chakra is imbalanced there are fears around survival: being provided for financially as well as family or group security.

Blockage in this area often happens following traumatic events, family problems, and major life changes. There may also be chronic lower back pain, sciatica, immune-related disorders, addictions, varicose veins, constipation, diarrhea, rectal/anal problems, impotence, water retention, and problems with groin, hips, legs, knees, calves, ankles, and feet.

When Reiki is performed at the root chakra, we have a better sense of feeling grounded and supported and begin to find relief from many of these chronic ailments.

2nd Chakra/*Sacral* Chakra - Sexuality & Creativity

This chakra is located about 1-2 inches below the navel. It is the chakra that deals with sex, power, money, gender, emotions, creativity, and procreation. When this chakra is imbalanced there might be lower back, pelvic or hip problems, Obstetrics/Gynecological imbalances (including fibroids, cysts, etc.) and issues around sexual potency, relationships, abundance, as well as power and control. This chakra is also linked to how we express our creativity and is related to the throat chakra.

Sexual abuse or trauma can create an energy block in this chakra. Reiki can help bring these deeply suppressed emotions to the surface, especially anger, allowing us to finally and fully heal.

3rd Chakra/*Solar Plexus* Chakra - Wisdom & Power

Located 1-2 inches above the navel, the solar plexus chakra is where we are connected to our self-esteem and self-protection. When we feel scattered and direct our energies outward, it is usually a sign that we have given our power away. When this happens, we might feel discomfort or a whirling sensation in the solar plexus chakra.

Physical imbalances may manifest as anorexia or bulimia, liver or adrenal dysfunction, fatigue, stomach ulcers, diabetes or indigestion.

Emotionally we may be afraid to step into our power, have issues around self-confidence, self-respect, and feel easily intimidated, weak, closed off or depressed. When Reiki is performed, and these blockages are removed...we've cleared the way to take action and make clear decisions in our life.

4th Chakra/*Heart* Chakra - Love & Healing

Located at the center of the chest, the heart chakra is how we tap into our higher selves: self-love, divine love, and consciousness. When it is imbalanced, we may physically experience heart issues like congestive heart failure or heart attacks, asthma/allergies, lung cancer, breast cancer, or bronchial pneumonia.

Emotionally we may lack compassion and feel lonely, disconnected from ourselves and others, resentful, depressed (due to lack of hope), grief, and distrustful of love. *Reiki opens us up to accept and allow love.*

5th Chakra/*Throat* Chakra - Communication

Located in the base of the throat, the throat chakra helps us to speak our truth. It deals with the issues of creativity, communication, and *the will to live*. Physical manifestation of this chakra's imbalances may show up as thyroid problems, TMJ, sore throat, swollen glands or scoliosis.

Emotional manifestations include being afraid of silence, fearful of being judged and rejected. Imbalances in this chakra can also be connected to addiction. When Reiki is performed to help clear this chakra, we are better able to express ourselves or follow our dreams.

6th Chakra/*Third Eye* - Awareness

Located between the eyebrows, the third eye chakra helps us see what is not physical. This is where our intuition lies, as well as clairvoyance and psychic perception. When this chakra is imbalanced, we may experience brain issues such as stroke, brain tumor/hemorrhage, neurological disturbances, and seizures. Emotionally, we do not trust our sights/visions or intuitions and may become afraid of them. Reiki can help unblock this chakra and allow us to hone-in-on the power of our intuition.

7th Chakra/*Crown* Chakra – Spirituality

Located above the head at the center of the crown this chakra is our connection to the Universe, our spirituality, and the ability to trust in life. This is the chakra from which we receive divine guidance from Source/Goddess/Higher Power. When this chakra is imbalanced, it manifests physically as depression or as chronic exhaustion that is not linked to physical disorders. Emotionally, we are unable to let go of anxiety and fear. There is also a lack of trust in the Universe/God or life.

When Reiki is performed, the 7th chakra becomes unblocked. This allows us to be more in touch with Divine guidance and have more trust in life.

Chakra Healing

Those who have been through toxic narcissistic relationships benefit tremendously with Reiki since it works with the mind-body as a whole. The pattern they have in common is the lack of self-esteem and self-love, which *is the significant key in their healing.*

Reiki energy will help clear out blocked energy pathways, promoting equilibrium in the body and a sense of feeling grounded with a deeper connection to the true self.

Focusing on the heart chakra, during a full body chakra balancing treatment, will greatly improve the emotional state of the client. The Reiki energy will open, energize, and balance the heart chakra. This energy will then be able to flow into the cells of the body. The cells in turn recognize this universal life energy and draw from it. By releasing the blocked energy at the heart chakra, the heart can heal. The piled-up anger, unforgiveness, and past pain will also resolve. As the heart strengthens it opens, allowing the true self to receive love.

Today, Reiki is one of the most effective and widely used complementary therapies. It is offered in hospitals, hospices, and private practices. Patients who receive Reiki often find they require less pain medication and spend less time recovering from illness. Dr. Oz's wife Lisa, a Reiki Master, stated in an interview: "The next wave of medical advances will be when we come to recognize the body as an energetic system."

As a person who has been exposed to the trauma and manipulation from an abusive relationship with a narcissist, Reiki ended up being a profound tool for my empowerment and personal healing. This growth has helped release the deeper and hidden wounds that I could not have reached alone with allopathic modalities. It was Quantum Medicine and healing that brought me through my healing journey. My personal journey with Reiki opened up my own gift to help others towards their healing.

Aromatherapy

Smell is the only one of our five senses that is directly linked to the lobe of the brain known as the Amygdala which houses our emotions and is shown to have a direct effect on the limbic system. Positive and negative emotions such as fear, anger, depression, and anxiety originate from this area. To access and release emotional trauma after a narcissistic relationship, we must stimulate the amygdala.

People turn to prescription drugs to find relief from anxiety, depression, PTSD (Post-traumatic Stress Disorder) and C-PTSD (Complex Post-Traumatic Stress Disorder). Due to the strange and unnatural design of pharmaceuticals, these medications will always disrupt other bodily functions. Thus, you will always have some side effects.

Unlike pharmaceuticals, aroma-therapeutic essential oils address symptoms at a cellular level by deleting misinformation and reprogramming correct information so that cells function properly and in harmony with one another. Suppressed emotions and memories can lead to anxiety, panic attacks, and depression.

Essential oils can help to release these emotions from where they are stored in our cells or energy field. Each oil has its own set of special properties. Essential oils can be combined and tailored to specific health concerns.

Aromatherapy is especially effective when used in conjunction with other healing modalities such as energy healing, guided meditation, and massage therapy.

Some of the most common and beneficial oils which aid in emotional healing are...

Lavender: Proven to be beneficial for anxiety, depression, irritability, panic attacks, and stress reduction. Researchers at the University of Miami found that inhalation of lavender oil enhanced beta waves in the brain, suggesting improved relaxation.

Roman Chamomile: Helps aid the release of stress from our mental, emotional, and physical bodies. It soothes our emotional wounds and has a virtuous quality. Therefore, it is also helpful for inner child work... particularly when addressing feelings of abandonment, which can be triggered during the course and the aftermath of toxic relationships.

Bergamot: This oil helps us in the areas of self-love, self-worth, self-acceptance, self-judgment, and self-loathing. It helps do the work necessary to step out of one's fears of not being good enough, and habits of holding back for fear of rejection. Bergamot instills validation within, allowing us to accept our own authenticity and not spend so much time worrying about the opinions of others.

Basil: Helpful in dealing with feelings of anxiety, panic or apprehension. Known as the oil of renewal, both emotionally and spiritually. It provides strength and tranquility to the heart and mind thus making it perfect for overwhelm, stress, and fatigue. It may even assist a person in their efforts to overcome addiction—which makes it a great choice for overcoming ruminating thoughts and self-sabotaging behaviors that often result from abusive relationships.

Meditation

There are many practices of health maintenance for the mind to prevent giving wrong meaning to situations. One of the main ones is meditation. The purpose of meditation is to slow down the mind. It enables us to not jump into a wrong meaning; instead we learn to deliberate before giving meaning to a situation. By practicing meditation stress, worry, and anxiety drops off and gives rise to a positive state of mind. In turn this has a positive impact on our physical body, brain, and nervous system. Some studies state that meditation for just 30 minutes a day can be as effective as the use of antidepressants.

Meditation gives us a sense of relaxation and enables us to heal physically, mentally, and spiritually. There are Harvard studies proving how meditation helps us to grow new connections within our brains. It decreases blood pressure and improves physical ailments. You really can get and stay healthier via meditation.

Statistically it is shown that women who have undergone abusive relationships have a higher incidence rate in cancer than all other post ailments. To heal she must take a *quantum leap* from her mind and its known mental representations of love, in order to rediscover the true value of love. Only then can quantum healing occur. Meditation is a key factor for reprogramming this thinking towards a positive state of mind and bringing forth mindfulness for this healing to occur.

Your mind can create healing energy. Positivity has a huge healing effect on the body. This is where Epigenetics comes in.

The little voice inside our head, the one that we never listened to is our consciousness.

As you meditate, you learn to believe that inner voice. You become more aware of your surroundings and your understandings as a whole. You experience more compassion for yourself and others. Meditation brings a deep sense of peace into the body. The things in your world become more trivial. You become more of yourself and you feel whole. Nothing else really bothers you anymore because you have more love and compassion for yourself.

Through meditation you develop the ability to respond rather than react. You become more like the Sage. Everything *just is* which really takes the drama out of your life. Having a deep understanding of oneself alleviates the need to respond.

Meditation allows you to move through life making decisions and taking action on those decisions, without being controlled by your emotions or ego. The *ego responses* lessen because you are confident. When you hear things that may be upsetting or annoying, you are more at peace within yourself so it's easier to just let go of the drama. If other people are bringing drama to you, you can easily pass it off as being filtered through their belief system and not yours.

Let Go of Attachments

We face many experiences, influences, and consequences in our life that dictate who we are or who we should be. Letting go of being attached to those concepts and realizing that we are enough can really grounds us. Having a partner or a flowing career can be satisfying and happy, yet that's not what defines us. It doesn't make us who we are. We must go deeper to understand that only *we* can make ourselves happy.

Our transformations teach, inspire, and bring strength to ourselves and others. No matter what, our life is not wasted.

Make sure to do the activities you used to enjoy, and the things that gave you pleasure.

You Have Your Life Back

Many people feel like they can never come out of a narcissistic relationship. They are too scared to even go back into the real world because their decision-making skills are weak. They feel like everything they did was wrong. This need not be the case.

Rather than going back to the person you were before... you will be starting a new life of emotional freedom, unlimited thinking, and overall well-being.

STORIES OF TRANSFORMATION

Women Who Got Their Life Back

The following stories of transformational healing and recovery are of women who have been involved in narcissistic relationships. These women have endured devastating emotional, physical, and psychological consequences through these relationships.

An observation scale of 1-10, based on progress, was used to assess these women. The components used in assessment were: Self-Esteem, Codependency, Anxiety & Fear, Confidence, Forgiveness, Self-Love, Assertiveness, Gratitude, Positive Thinking, and Mindfulness. *This study was based on client feed-back and the observational level of healing experience they had seen within one year of solid commitment.* Quantum Based Life Coaching, Energy Work, and other Quantum modalities specifically: Aromatherapy and Emotional Freedom Technique (EFT) were used in each case. This resulted in a positive lifestyle change as well as healing physical, mental, and spiritual damage. Ninety-five percent healing was achieved with longevity and adherence. It is seen that the Quantum Medicinal Approach in Life Coaching and Energy Work facilitates the healing of women affected by abusive narcissistic relationships.

The positive results seen in these women stress the importance of Quantum modalities in energy healing for the relief and achievement of gaining a happy, peaceful, and loving lifestyle... without fear or resurrection of the aftermath from abuse.

Meet Stephanie

A 43-year-old female, who we will call Stephanie, came into my office feeling hopeless and sad. She had recently separated from her narcissistic husband of 7 years where she was exposed to tremendous emotional, verbal, and psychological trauma. It took almost two years for her to gain enough courage to end her relationship. She had a 3-year-old from this marriage and two children from her previous marriage, a 10-year-old and 12-year old who also lived with her.

Vocation: Digital Marketing Analyst

Stephanie worked in a prestigious company in the city. She is beautiful, educated, financially stable, and carries herself well. Stephanie stated that she was highly respected for her accomplishments in her company and despite being well liked by her colleagues, she didn't have many friends. For the past few years, Stephanie had been scared to associate with her co-workers in an "out of work" environment because her husband would get suspicious of her whereabouts. She found his demeanor to be nerve wracking and exhausting. Stephanie would give an excuse to her colleagues that she had a busy social and family life and couldn't easily commit to social events. Stephanie didn't have friends of her own, as her husband's friends had become her friends... despite him not having any real friends himself.

In his eyes, friends were a waste of time. She stated that she had pushed away the few close friends that she had, since her husband felt they were a bad influence around her and didn't like their character despite having a charismatic and charming disposition towards them when he would be in their presence.

Her friends had questioned her change of character when she was around her husband, stating she appeared as a puppet without an opinion, which is unlike the opinionated captivating persona she had most of her life. Stephanie didn't want to deal with her friend's scrutiny or the backlash from her husband, so she had stopped associating with them. In her eyes this was another chance to create a successful marriage, especially with this brilliant magnetic man. Stephanie was determined, as she said, "to make this happen." She mentioned that her friends couldn't possibly understand how she felt and how important this was for her. She stated, "They don't understand him like I do."

She also stated that she felt suddenly alone.

Her parents live only 45 minutes away and her brother and his family lives about 2 hours from her. She hadn't told them the truth about her marriage or exhibited any signs that there were any problems. In fact, she felt that they would probably blame her for her *failed marriages*. When her first marriage was going into a divorce, she recalled her mother asking, "What was going on with you that made him (her ex-husband) stray?"

Stephanie had a hard time concentrating and her self-esteem was tattered. As she was speaking, she would constantly do self-talk creating solutions. She would speak out about possible *maybes* or how if she had done certain things differently, she could have avoided certain repercussions of a given situation or scenario.

Her mind was constantly reeling to find answers on why all this had happened to her. She stated multiple times during our initial sessions, "I can understand it happening once (her marriage going into a divorce), but twice? Something must be wrong with me. I tried so very hard to do everything correct, but nothing has been good enough."

Despite Stephanie taking an initiative to end the relationship, she was deeply confused. She was confident that she couldn't continue to live in or subject her children to the toxicity of her marriage. She was also holding on to the idea that maybe she could have done something different to bring about a change in her spouse in order to save her marriage. Stephanie felt responsible for the so-called *failure* even though the marriage was torturous.

Stephanie's Musings: "The main reason I stayed was because I was afraid. I was afraid of dealing with another failed marriage, afraid of the future, afraid of being single again, afraid of never being able to find anyone else and ending up alone with three children from two different fathers. I didn't want that social stigma. My life was not supposed to end up like this. I stayed on because he made me feel like I was screwed up and difficult and that no one else but him would be able to love me or put up with me. My ex-husband couldn't stomach me and ran off with different women behind my back saying I didn't fulfill him. I felt Gary (current husband) was giving me another chance. He loves my other two children like his own. Where would I find someone that loving towards my kids that aren't theirs? "

The fear and the high self-made bar, the standard of equating success as being happily married, gripped her to the core. Her low self-esteem from her previous marriage had altered her sense of thinking where she was convinced, by her current husband, that she was the cause of all their problems. Her need for his acceptance allowed him to manipulate. She had given up all control of her life in order to feed his narcissistic egoic thinking. She also avoided any confrontation, which satisfied her codependent nature.

The emotional and psychological abuse left her a complete empty shell of a being. She was convinced that having her marriage fall apart signified that she was a failure to herself, her kids, extended family, and society despite knowing her husband was toxic to her and her children.

Before coming to me, Stephanie had been undergoing psychotherapy consistently for 18 months. She felt it had been helpful and yet she also knew that she was nowhere close to recovery. She had been separated for over a year and her divorce had been filed.

Stephanie's Primary Care Physician had prescribed her Ambien 5mg (Zolpidem) to help her with her insomnia. This drug made her feel drowsy and less energetic upon waking up in the morning. She desperately wanted to stop her sleep medications.

As an Assertiveness Life Coach using the Quantum Healing Approach, I first discussed with Stephanie about formulating a positive intent to bring forth creativity and manifestation. Together in our sessions, the emphasis was towards mind–body healing, working on her self-esteem, setting boundaries, as well as forgiveness of others and self.

We discussed the positive intent of looking towards an abundant future. Forgiving and letting go of the past hurt, pain, and disrespect with an understanding that forgiveness is important more for herself than her abuser. During her initial session we focused on reprogramming her mind in order to gain freedom from self-imposed standards, while removing fears and negativity. Reprogramming her mind also included loving herself for the person she is...which is *perfectly imperfect*...like all human beings.

We did one Guided Meditation, which taught Stephanie the ability to slow down her mind in order to prevent it from giving an inaccurate meaning to a given situation. This significantly helped Stephanie to conquer and remove her fears. I also conducted a Reiki Energy Healing during her initial session. Blockages were seen throughout all 7 of her chakras and most heavily in her heart, solar plexus, sacral, and root.

I worked on the alignment and removal of the blockages. She was amazed at how much better and whole she felt as if a weight had been lifted off her. Stephanie let me know that her mind did not feel as clouded. This brought her hope and in turn some positive intention. She continued with her weekly sessions of Life Coaching, Meditation, and Reiki for 6 continuous months.

Now Stephanie can meditate on her own for 20 minutes every day unguided. Her mind doesn't wander anymore, nor does she sound flighty when she speaks. Positive clarity in her thinking increased her confidence towards her decision-making skills and her fears have dissipated, being replaced by her increased sense of awareness towards living in the moment. She began to trust herself.

The weekly Reiki energy work significantly helped Stephanie's healing process where her stresses and anxieties have mostly disappeared. Her energy system is more balanced with a clearer aura and self-love. She has understood the importance of loving and forgiving herself. She now believes that she is deserving. This brought about positive growth out of her codependency. She understands that she is enough and there is no need to receive validations from a partner to understand her worth.

Stephanie stated that she now has a sense of peace and calm that she hadn't felt for years. She no longer takes any medications for sleep and has stopped her psychotherapy on her own will with collaboration of her therapist. Stephanie has reached out to her family and friends again and is slowly incorporating everyone back into her life. She now enjoys sitting down and spending time with her children and being more mindful to enjoy and connect with them in the moment.

Stephanie continues Reiki energy healing work with me twice a month and attends my Group Guided Meditation classes to raise her vibrations further towards positivity and manifestation.

OBSERVATIONAL ASSESSMENT (1-10)

Stephanie	INITIAL CONSULT	6 MONTH CONSULT
SELF-ESTEEM	1	9
CODEPENDENCY	8	1
ANXIETY & FEAR	10	2
CONFIDENCE	2	8
FORGIVENESS	1	9
SELF-LOVE	4	9
ASSERTIVENESS	4	8
GRATITUDE	2	9
POSITIVE THINKING AND MINDFULLNESS	1	9

MY SOULMATE MY LOVE MY NARCISSIST

Meet Sarah

Sarah, as we will call her, is a 44-year-old Computer Software Engineer who recently divorced her husband of 13 years. She has two sons aged 10 and 8 who live with her. Sarah met her ex-husband at a time in her life where she was at the top of her career in a Fortune 500 company. She owned her own home along with other investments and assets.

When they met, her now ex-husband was coming out of a claimed "terrible nightmare of a relationship" where he was treated without any dignity or respect and felt used. He explained to Sarah that for some reason he just kept "picking the wrong women" and "can't seem to catch a break." He confided in her about his childhood, where his mother had left him when he was five years old and so he was raised by an abusive alcoholic father. He explained that he was looking to find someone nice to settle down with and start a family. Sarah felt sympathy towards him and understood. She admired the fact that he was established in his career, carried himself well, and was extremely charming. He went to church and he always caught everyone's attention with his charismatic personality and smile.

A whirlwind romance began where Sarah was showered with gifts, flowers, love notes, and surprises. He took effort and care towards every little detail for her, making her feel special. This man wanted the same things as her in life. She was overjoyed as she felt she had finally met her soulmate, and within 6 months they were married.

After the wedding, red flags started to appear. Within 3 months his true identity and insecurities showed up. He was extremely possessive in nature and didn't like Sarah being out of his site. Soon Sarah became isolated from her friends and family... followed by the devaluing phase of rejection, manipulation, abuse, and control.

Whenever her husband felt that Sarah might attempt to leave, his switch would come back on with the crying and begging for her forgiveness. He would make her feel guilty by asking her not to leave him like his mother did and promised to change. The love bombing would begin again, giving Sarah hope and security.

Eventually Sarah was manipulated to quit her job in order to stay home and raise their children. She sold her home that she owned and had no access to bank accounts for money. Her husband controlled everything. He would give her a weekly allowance in which she was accounted for by showing him receipts and the items she may have bought for the house, herself or the kids.

Sarah's strong Christian belief that a good wife always stood by their husband and the fact that divorce was biblically incorrect, tortured her. She also justified and made excuses for her husband's actions because of his abusive childhood and all he needed in her mind was 'a little extra love and attention to allow him to feel secure' which would save him and their marriage.

Sarah eventually became depressed and lost herself during this process. She understood she needed help and started to go for counselling. After a year of counseling she decided to end her marriage, took her children and left.

When Sarah came to me, she felt broken and filled with despair despite being divorced and going through counseling for two years.

Sarah's Musings: "I stayed with my husband because he needed me. I felt it was my job to stand by him. I stayed because I was 'supposed to' and that was the right thing to do since we had children. I left because I realized I was teaching my sons to disrespect women by allowing myself to be treated this way."

Sarah came to me through a recommendation from another client and even though she felt this was against her religious belief, she still gravitated to make the appointment.

Sarah had undergone Cognitive Behavioral Therapy, EMDR (Eye Movement Desensitization and Reprocessing), worked on her self-esteem, boundaries, and forgiveness with guidance from her psychotherapist. Sarah also saw an allopathic physician who had suggested two different anti-depressant pills. She did not want to begin medications. Sarah states that she felt better from when she had first left her husband, and yet she didn't understand why her recovery was taking so long. She felt there must be something she was not doing or there was something that she was missing.

I explained to Sarah that she didn't have to disassociate her beliefs in-regards to religion and her healing process. In fact, the power of prayer for healing alone brings forth positive intentions, where we communicate our thoughts, send out positive vibrations to the universal aspect of God or higher consciousness to be brought into manifestation.

Sarah became more comfortable with this newfound knowledge and her first session began on a positive and comfortable note. Together we created positive intentions and she prayed, thus formulating a tangled hierarchy. In our Life Coaching sessions, I emphasized the importance of mind–body healing. We worked on repairing her self-esteem by utilizing Reiki energy to balance her solar plexus chakra, setting out strict boundaries and forgiveness for others and self. Sarah understood through our sessions that forgiving and letting go of past hurt and pain is important more for herself, than her abuser.

After the coaching sessions, we did Guided Meditation and Reiki energy healing work. I incorporated Aromatherapy using a mixture of Lavender and Bergamot essential oils to help aid in anxiety and stress relief. These essential oils are powerful adjuvants in the healing process of anxiety and depression. This was to help Sarah release emotions from where they were stored in her cells and in her energy fields.

Sarah found a surprised sense of peace and wholeness from her first session alone. As the sessions continued, we focused on reprogramming her mind from any negative conditioning in order to remove fears or self-imposed exiles towards trust and love.

Sarah dedicated 8 months to her healing journey on a weekly basis with diligence. Her positivity grew and the despair she once claimed that was "eating her up inside" was gone. She no longer felt broken and forgiveness had come much easier due to her increase in awareness, clarity, and mindfulness. Guided Meditation and Reiki helped her by aligning her heart, solar plexus, and root chakras... which were significantly blocked. As we continued with Reiki, she felt the release of negative patterns and energy. This relieved most of her anxieties and stress. She enjoyed the Aromatherapy which brought great comfort and stress relief. Sarah became more in tune with her inner self. This developed her confidence and raised her self-esteem. She learned to appreciate and love herself.

Sarah found a new job and had accepted her new role as a single mom. She enjoys and relishes every minute of her parenting and is happy that her mind can now focus on the moments she has with her children. Sarah continues with meditation as well as Reiki energy work at least once a month. This allows her to continue her spiritual path and healing.

OBSERVATIONAL ASSESSMENT (1-10)

Sarah	INITIAL CONSULT	6 MONTH CONSULT
SELF-ESTEEM	3	8
CODEPENDENCY	7	2
ANXIETY & FEAR	8	2
CONFIDENCE	4	7
FORGIVENESS	2	9
SELF-LOVE	2	7
ASSERTIVENESS	4	7
GRATITUDE	2	9
POSITIVE THINKING AND MINDFULLNESS	1	9

MY SOULMATE MY LOVE MY NARCISSIST

Meet Jackie

A 28-year-old woman, who we will call Jackie, came to my office feeling lost. Jackie had been divorced for the past 6 months. Her children were ages 7 and 5 and they resided with her.

Jackie had married her high school sweetheart. He was the only man she had ever known. In high school, her now ex-husband, was the football quarterback and was very popular and charming. He was the center of attention and always caught people's eye wherever he went. He sought after Jackie with a full onset of love bombing, calling her 10-20 times a day, as well as showering her with gifts and flowers. They were very young, but she was convinced that no man could ever love her like he did. He was obsessed with her. She perceived this obsession as flattery and reveled in it. Jackie felt proud to be his girlfriend and was convinced he was her soulmate.

Despite the advice from her family and even though they were young, a year down the road they decided to get married. It wasn't very far into their marriage that she noticed his behavior had started to change. Soon the honeymoon period was over. Her so-called soulmate became cold, detached, and highly critical.

The devaluation stage had begun and no matter what Jackie did to *make him love her again...* it would only set him off in an angry rage or he would accuse her of being a liar, a cheat or a manipulator. Jackie constantly walked on eggshells in fear of setting him off and into a rage.

Jackie never finished college. Her husband had convinced her that their finances could be put to better use than her schooling. Jackie decided to stay home and raise her children. Due to her husband's possessiveness, she became isolated from her friends and family.

Jackie was not allowed to have access to their finances. She was told that she was irresponsible and liked to *blow all his money*.

Eventually she discovered that her husband was having an affair and felt devastated. She didn't understand how her charming soulmate could look for happiness outside of their marriage. When asked... her husband would vehemently deny the affair and manipulated the situation by accusing Jackie of being paranoid, overly sensitive or dramatic.

Initially Jackie believed she was the cause of his infidelity and took on self-blame. After multiple affairs, she decided to leave him for good. With great difficulty and courage, Jackie took her children and moved back to her parent's home where her family helped her with the children so she could get on her own feet. She started a job working part time at a doctors' office as a scheduler and is considering going back to school.

Jackie's Musings: "I stayed two years longer than I should have because he was my first love. He was charming and kind when he wasn't sleeping with other people behind my back. I had trusted him more than you can imagine, and I was scared to leave him since he was the only means of financial support for myself and the children. I had dedicated my whole life to him and our kids... and now I don't know how to function, because everything had been about him."

Jackie came to my office stating that she couldn't get control of her mind. She felt very anxious at times. Every time she thought back to all the terrible and hurtful events she went through with her ex-husband, Jackie felt as though it had just happened yesterday. She couldn't shake it off. When she went to work, she felt scared to speak to people, and couldn't hold a conversation without feeling like she wanted to go home and hide in her room.

I sat with Jackie and together we discussed what her ideal life would be like using the Quantum Approach towards healing. She visualized herself happy and most importantly at peace. We discussed the importance of forgiveness where forgiveness is not only about forgiving the other individual, but most importantly to forgive ourselves for allowing these events to happen.

We spoke about growth in self-esteem, self-love, and Quantum healing through Reiki, Guided Meditation, and Chakra healing. I told her about the chakra energy centers of our body and how important it is to reprogram the body cells to unlearn the negative, bringing in positive energy for healing and recovery.

During her initial session, Guided Meditation brought Jackie to a relaxed state. Her throat, heart, solar plexus, and root chakras had severe blockages. Reiki cleared and stabilized her energy. She stated during the Reiki session she had vivid visions and saw blue and purple colors. I used various Quartz crystals in order to amplify the healing energy. I showed her some specific EFT techniques that she could use at home in order to neutralize and maintain her energy.

During the meditation process her mind was initially racing. Midway through, Jackie couldn't believe how her mind had stilled, giving her a sense of peace. She felt these were all very positive signs as she began her healing journey.

Jackie decided to commit to coming to my office once a week for the next 5 months. She had remarkable changes within herself and could feel the strength in the healing that had taken place. She became more mindful and was able to stay fully present. If a past memory came into her thoughts, she did not re-live the pain anymore. She was able to see her past as a life lesson.

Jackie got stronger. She became more loving and able to feel peace within herself.

It is pleasant to see how Jackie has evolved and when she attends the group meditations, she brings along pleasant, positive love energy.

OBSERVATIONAL ASSESMENT (1-10)

Jackie	INITIAL CONSULT	6 MONTH CONSULT
SELF-ESTEEM	1	7
CODEPENDENCY	10	2
ANXIETY & FEAR	10	3
CONFIDENCE	2	9
FORGIVENESS	1	8
SELF-LOVE	1	9
ASSERTIVENESS	0	7
GRATITUDE	1	8
POSITIVE THINKING AND MINDFULLNESS	2	9

Meet Riya

A 27-year-old divorced woman of one year, who we will call Riya, came to my office stating that she felt very anxious and sad. Riya explained that her family comes from a strong, culturally influenced Indian society here in the United States. Despite herself being born and raised here, she had allowed her culture to influence many decisions which she felt had not benefited her life.

Riya had finished medical school, three years prior to coming to me, and had been matched into a residency. Her parents were searching for a prospective groom for her to meet, despite Riya explaining to them that she wasn't ready for marriage until after she had completed her residency.

According to her parents' society and culture, she was already beyond *marriageable age* and her parents insisted that she meet some prospective grooms. A son from a wealthy diamond business owner was one proposal prospect they introduced to her. He didn't have much of an education, but he helped in the family business. Riya decided to meet this man and he turned out to be very charming and handsome.

During their courtship, he showered her with flowers, cards, and expensive jewelry. He would even surprise her with beautiful expensive gifts at her hospital. Riya became the envy of all her nurses, and she felt star-struck in love. Within three months and with her consent, their families agreed on the marriage. She was to move in with his family after the wedding and she would continue her residency at the hospital.

Within the first week after their wedding, Riya noticed her new husband's behavior changing. He had become increasingly possessive and demanded an explanation for every call or text she would receive. He began to criticize what she wore and felt she was exposing herself on purpose in order to receive attention from other men. The verbal abuse was consuming her and eventually he manipulated her to the point where she became isolated from her family and friends.

Riya tried to reach out to her mother and her aunts for advice regarding his behavior. They all took it very lightly and explained to her that this was *normal* and how divorce is considered a social embarrassment. One of her aunts specifically reprimanded Riya.

As the year passed, her husband became deplorable with his behavior. Day-by-day Riya felt like she was slowly losing her mind. She didn't understand how her husband who was extremely loving one day, showering her with gifts and pleasantries, could be cruel and demeaning the next. Her self-esteem was tattered, and she walked on eggshells around him. It was on one of his off days as Riya was getting ready for work that her husband went into a rage. He took her purse, knowing that her cell phone and car keys were inside it, and left. He purposely sabotaged her means to go to work as he knew she would get kicked out of the residency program. Riya's entire life had been dedicated to Medicine.

This was a real eye-opener for her and confirmed her need to leave.

The next day her husband apologized, professing his love to her and wanting her back. Riya finally broke the cycle and left him. Her family disowned her and, not too long after her divorce, her now-ex-husband remarried.

Riya had a very negative outlook on life when she came to me. She was very anxious, filled with anger, and felt betrayed. She could not grasp how her ex-husband and her own family had both displayed love to her yet found her disposable at the same time. She felt alone and exhausted.

Riya was undergoing therapy with a psychiatrist who had put her on Zoloft (Sertraline) to help her with her anxiety, as well as Ambien (Zolpidem) for sleep. She felt these meds weren't helping her. She still couldn't sleep at night, her body felt heavy, and her mind was constantly racing.

I explained to her the importance of taking each experience in life as a lesson to reach for her highest good and soul purpose.

After the initial two sessions of life coaching, I did Energy work using Reiki and Guided Meditation. We incorporated Aromatherapy using a combination of Lavender, Roman Chamomile, and Basil. All three of these essential oils were powerful additions to her healing process. These oils relieve anxiety and depression by helping to release emotions from where they are stored in our cells and energy fields.

I was able to assess that her heart and solar plexus chakras were blocked and concentrated on these areas for release and alignment. Riya felt a remarkable difference during her first session alone and was surprised to feel so relaxed. She stated that she felt lighter as if her burdens had come off her shoulders. She felt emotional after the session which is expected due to the release and healing that takes place within the energy field.

Riya continued her sessions for the next 6 months on a weekly basis. After 6 months Riya regained her positive outlook on life. She concluded that what her family does, will not affect her as she only needs herself for validation. She understands that her family's priorities depend more on *what others think* than what *they feel themselves*. She now sees this as *their way of life* and the *only way they know* how to function. This has helped Riya to make peace with it all.

She has forgiven herself and those who have hurt her. She's in a happier place in her life with her increased self-confidence, awareness, and spirituality. She now comes a minimum of once a month for her sessions and has stopped all psychotherapy and medications. Riya is also enjoying her new, healthy patterns of sleep.

OBSERVATIONAL ASSESMENT (1-10)

Riya	INITIAL CONSULT	6 MONTH CONSULT
SELF-ESTEEM	1	8
CODEPENDENCY	9	1
ANXIETY & FEAR	9	1
CONFIDENCE	2	9
FORGIVENESS	0	9
SELF-LOVE	2	10
ASSERTIVENESS	4	9
GRATITUDE	0	9
POSITIVE THINKING AND MINDFULLNESS	0	10

Meet Susan

Susan, as we will call her, a 28-year-old who met her narcissistic boyfriend at age 20 while in college. He was working as a dorm room assistant and Susan felt very drawn to him. She was very shy and eventually drew up the courage to contact him via social media. They started an internet romance and would chat all hours of the night via computer or phone.

When she got tired and wanted to get off the phone or computer with him, to go to sleep, he would get angry at her. Eventually Susan discovered that he was very arrogant and judgmental. He acted as though everyone was below him. He was very controlling and constantly picked fights with her.

What bothered her the most was that in the evenings, he would meet her in private and during the day he would walk right past her without any acknowledgement. When she would get back to her room, she would find messages from him asking how her day had been. Susan found this to be confusing and when she would ask him, he would just state that *he wanted to keep the relationship private for now.*

Susan's Musings: "I was always there for him. All he had to do was shoot me a text and I would be by his side, then he'd ignore me again. This vicious cycle of *pulling me in and casting me out*, lasted for seven-and-half years. I tried so hard to be everything he wanted me to be, the bar was always raised a bit higher. My life turned into a constant leaping for something that I would never reach. I remember sobbing to myself on a daily basis. I was extremely depressed and went to the doctor to beg him to put me on something to make me feel better. I was prescribed an antidepressant and two anxiety medications."

In between, Susan tried to break away by dating other men. As soon as he recognized she was happy, he would lure her right back in with promises and hope. This eventually turned into a form of punishment where he felt she deserved the negative treatment. She was considered untrustworthy in his eyes since she dated other men, and to redeem herself she would have to do sexual acts that she did not feel comfortable doing with him. If she refused, she was not *worthy* of him, and he would discard her by not speaking to her for several weeks. He would refuse her phone calls and not answer any of her texts. This would leave her feeling hurt and obsessed. She felt like she was going crazy.

Susan came to me stating she was living in fear and was in a great deal of pain. Her narcissistic boyfriend had refused her phone calls for the past three weeks. She felt so lost and hurt that she just couldn't function or even get out of bed. She told me that she wanted all of this to stop so she could get her life back.

Using the Quantum Approach in Life Coaching and Healing, I sat down and explained to her the different modalities of Quantum healing I could do with her. I also made sure she understood the No Contact rule. This would be her biggest hurdle and I knew it would hurt initially. I also knew that this would make her stronger.

Susan came to me twice a week for the first 2 months where we concentrated on Quantum based Life Coaching, Guided Meditation, and Reiki using Aromatherapy. I used Bergamot and Lavender Essential Oils. Some days I would add Basil or Roman Chamomile, depending on the energy. I would intuitively pick up from Susan how to help her release emotions which were stored in her cells and in her energy fields.

The initial Guided Meditation and Reiki session was impactful and emotional. This experience brought forth much-needed releases from the negative pattern she was involved in. Susan had blockages throughout all 7 of her chakras and more heavily in her heart, solar plexus, sacral, and root chakras. I worked on the alignment and removal of these blockages. At the end of the session, she had a sense of peace and thus began her healing journey to strengthen her inner core and to gain mindfulness for positive thinking.

After a few sessions, she could actually feel the pain leave her body and she felt lighter. Peaceful thoughts would enter her mind more often as opposed to thinking of the worst. As she continued her sessions, Susan gained more clarity and understanding. She became more aware of her own inner thoughts and the false beliefs that lead to her codependency. We continued to work on chakra clearing and alignment. Soon she felt well enough to come off her medications on her own accord.

Susan stopped experiencing the urge to connect with this man anymore. Her anger, pain, and resentment abated.

Today Susan walks with a newfound confidence, peace, and resilience. She let go of all that did not serve her, and she embraced the spirituality that has entered her life. She is grateful to finally gain back her power through healing and lives each moment with gratitude.

MY SOULMATE MY LOVE MY NARCISSIST

OBSERVATIONAL ASSESMENT (1-10)

Susan	INITIAL CONSULT	6 MONTH CONSULT
SELF-ESTEEM	0	8
CODEPENDENCY	10	2
ANXIETY & FEAR	10	2
CONFIDENCE	1	8
FORGIVENESS	1	9
SELF-LOVE	2	8
ASSERTIVENESS	1	8
GRATITUDE	0	9
POSITIVE THINKING AND MINDFULLNESS	0	10

MY SOULMATE MY LOVE MY NARCISSIST

OBERVATIONAL STUDY OVERALL AVERAGE OF IMPROVEMENT WITHIN 6 MONTHS				
	Stephanie %	Sarah %	Jackie %	Riya %	Susan %
SELF-ESTEEM	90	80	70	80	80
CODEPENDENCY	90	80	80	90	80
ANXIETY & FEAR	80	80	70	90	80
CONFIDENCE	80	70	90	90	80
FORGIVENESS	90	90	80	90	90
SELF-LOVE	90	70	90	90	80
ASSERTIVENESS	80	70	70	90	80
GRATITUDE	90	90	80	90	90
POSITIVE THINKING MINDFULNESS	90	90	90	100	100

Women who have been through narcissistic abusive relationships do not need to continuously suffer as they are trying to move forward to start a new life for themselves. These women deserve to live a life of peace, love, and gratitude; a life filled with self-love, confidence, and spirituality.

	Stephanie %	Sarah %	Jackie %	Riya %	Susan %
OVERALL AVERAGE OF IMPROVEMENT IN 6 MONTHS	87%	80%	80%	90%	84%

Quantum Medicine provides a curative approach
for this achievement.

A NOTE FROM THE AUTHOR

Our life journey is what makes us who we are today. As a medical physician, my life was always led by science. I wouldn't accept or see anything beyond this. I was very left brained. Despite always being intuitively correct, I would just brush it off as coincidence. Somewhere in my gut I knew it was something out of the ordinary and it wasn't just luck. When I read the book "Many Lives, Many Masters," by Dr. Brian Weiss, I finally understood how my own intuition wasn't just luck or coincidence.

Here was another medical physician, trained from Yale Medical School, an Ivy League college. He is the former chairman of psychiatry at Mt. Sinai Medical Center in Miami, Florida. With a renowned career in medicine, he's written several science-based research publications. One day as he was practicing hypnotherapy on one of his patients, he tapped into their past lives. I thought wow, maybe there is more that I need to learn and understand?

Like me, everything in Dr. Weiss' life was based on science. To date, he and his wife have done amazing healing work all over the world. He's been a guest on Oprah and worked with famous healers like Deepak Chopra and Dr. Wayne Dyer.

Dr. Weiss' work opened up a new world for me, so I sought him out and got trained by him to become a Past Life Regression therapist. I also became a Reiki Master and did my Doctorate in Natural Medicine.

I did my PhD in Integrative Medicine where I now work in the area of toxic relationships and the healing recovery of narcissistic victim abuse. I also enjoy bringing science into the mental health field to show how effective mindfulness and meditation can be.

Harvard studies have proven that grey matter can have a rebirth and we can grow new neural pathways. This is another way that we can heal. I do this so that the science world can incorporate my knowledge in order to help people heal. It's been quite the journey.

I am a single mother of four. As of writing this book, my children range in age from seventeen to six years old. I myself have been exposed to toxic narcissism in marriage.

Over the years I have met and heard about many people who have suffered or who are still suffering in a toxic relationship with a narcissistic partner. Despite their own better judgment and reality, many continue to stay in these abusive relationships. It is especially astonishing to see how many educated, financially independent, and extremely well-established women succumb to such abuse.

For those outside of a narcissistic relationship it is very difficult to conceive or to be empathetic towards the plight of these people. The obvious question would be, "Why would anyone put themselves through such pain and misery from another human being? If you're being hurt, abused or unhappy… why don't you just leave?"

Unfortunately, this thinking isn't so simple because it's not about logic and reasoning.

When I look back, I can see how I was entangled in this dark cloud of despair and illusion. I felt completely alone, although I didn't logically consider myself alone at all. I was desperate to save the relationship and yet there was nothing tangible to save.

These experiences remind me of a famous quote by American actor Robin Williams "I used to think that the worst thing in life was to end up alone. It's not. The worst thing in life is to end up with people who make you feel alone."

I was completely manipulated and controlled without being aware of being so and I eventually lost my entire sense of self.

There was no one in my life who could understand what I was going through at the time. When I reflect back, I wish I had known someone who knew 'what I know today' in order to help me. That person would have saved me a lot of confusion and suffering.

Only someone who has been through it can understand the gravity and spirit-crushing state you enter when you're involved with a narcissist. Words alone cannot describe the confusion, pain, and mental anguish we feel. We have no clue what hit us, and we don't easily comprehend what we are even involved in. The isolation and sense of being alone causes deep desperation. We tend to end up being far removed from any stable norm of life or reality.

The constant see-sawing cycle a person goes through in a narcissistic relationship will eventually leave the victim as an empty shell of themselves. The severe amount of post-traumatic stress, during and afterwards, is horrific in and of itself.

Psychotherapy and medication alone cannot bring complete healing. Therefore, I incorporate mindset reprogramming tools and use Quantum modalities of healing such as Mindfulness, Meditation, Reiki, and Energy work. My clients achieve concrete results and begin to live sustainable lives of peace and happiness.

I can understand and resonate with what my clients are going through, not only because I'm an empath... it's because I was that person once. My passion is to bring more focused awareness and healing to the world.

I Love Giving Back to My Community

My parents are both from Kerala, India and arrived here in New York around the late '70s to make their own life. They both were the eldest of the family and they each had 8-9 siblings that were younger. They didn't have much in the beginning but worked hard to provide for their family back in India. My parents educated their siblings, supported them to get married, and brought them all to the United States. They initially provided for their siblings to start their lives here and this was done with no expectations in return.

Many may say that in a cultural aspect it was their duty, but I know as humans when we are struggling ourselves to build a life it is difficult to help others.

My parents did it because they had a heart and wanted to give their siblings the opportunity to have a better life. They sacrificed for so many people and I learned at a very young age how powerful love and compassion can be.

Keynote Speaker

I have been a keynote speaker as well as chaired scientific events for global conferences and world congresses. At each and every one of them, when I discuss toxic abuse with a narcissistic partner, there's always this *A-ha moment*. I can see it in their eyes.

ABOUT THE AUTHOR

Author Dr. Bindu Babu is a successful Integrative Physician & Celebrity Transformational Coach who has mentored under Dr. Brian Weiss, MD and worked with other great quantum healers such as Dr. Paul Drouin, Dr. Amit Goswami, and Dr. Bruce Lipton. These men further deepened the connection between science and healing in her own life. Dr. Babu was awarded New York's Most Powerful Women in Business 2019. She is a Global Goodwill Ambassador, USA and Global Peace Chain Ambassador, USA. Dr. Babu is an honored member of the Circle of Wise Women - Female Wave of Change International. She has taken on the role of Organizing Committee Member & Chair at various psychiatry-based World Congresses and Global Summits, where she is a renowned international keynote speaker on narcissism and abusive toxic relationships.

Dr. Babu is also the Director of Leadership Academy for the New American Voters Association, a non-profit organization in New York. She has been nominated for the Wintrade Global 2020 Entrepreneur in Health & Wellness Award, UK and the 2020 iWomen Global Award, India. She was featured in the Formidable Women Magazine 2020 Spring issue and The Hollywood Times. Dr. Babu has spoken at prestigious universities such as Harvard and NYU and has been invited on many radio shows, podcasts, and live television talk shows throughout her career. Dr. Babu's office is in the Financial District, Manhattan, New York and she also works remotely with her clients worldwide.

TESTIMONIALS

"Dr Bindu Babu was very compassionate and honest. She took her time and explained her credentials to me and how she found her passion in helping others heal. She made sure I was comfortable before starting out my session and did not rush me to leave. She followed up with me after the session via email. I can't wait to set another appointment with her." ~Farah M.

"I feel so thankful to have met Dr. Bindu Babu. I have had coaching sessions with her. Dr. Babu's integrated approach helped me open my mind, providing me with actionable clarity which has enabled me to grow. Dr. Babu is incredibly intuitive and has made such a positive impact on every aspect of my life. I can't thank her enough." ~Diana L.

"I have always wanted to try meditation. I knew I was in good hands right away with Dr. Bindu Babu. I experienced her Guided Meditation and Reiki session. Dr. Babu is warm, friendly, and open. It was hard for me to clear my mind... with her guidance I was able to focus. I felt it not only mentally, but physically as well. I'm going to return and make this a part of my life. Reiki is phenomenal and I think everyone in the world could use a little bit of mindfulness right now. Beautiful experience. So happy and can't wait to return!" ~Elena D.

"From the moment I walked in I felt so comfortable and invited. The guided mediation put me in the most relaxed state. I felt like I was floating on air. The Reiki healing was very powerful and her message to me at the end of it had me in tears. I am so happy I made this appointment. I left feeling very hopeful about my life and my journey. Will be seeing her again soon." ~Stefanie B.

MY SOULMATE MY LOVE MY NARCISSIST

REFERENCES

68 Alcantera, Margarita (2014) Reiki 101: What Is It & Will I Love It? MindBodyGreen.com

Retrieved from http://www.mindbodygreen.com/0-15046/reiki-101-what-is-it-will-i-love-it.html

69 Dale, C (2015) Chakra Fundamentals and Basic Practices. Llewellyn's Complete Book of Chakras: Your Definitive Source of Energy Center Knowledge for Health, Happiness, and Spiritual Evolution: Section 1

52 Goswami, Amit PhD (2011) The Quantum Doctor: A Quantum Physicist Explains the Healing Power of Integral Medicine. Ch. 2-6

65 Goswami, Amit PhD (2013) Health, Healing and Quantum Physics.

Retrieved from: Amit Goswami.org
<http://www.amitgoswami.org/2013/08/13/health-healing-quantum-physics/>

66 Goswami, Amit PhD (2015)

Retrieved from:
http://www.amitgoswami.org/2013/08/05/quantum psychology/

69 Kilgore, Roberta (2016) Reiki for Traumatic Stress Relief. International Association of Reiki Professionals

Retrieved from: http://iarp.org/reiki-for-traumatic-stress-relief/

49 Lam, Michael, MD, MPH & Lam, D, RDN, MS, MPH (2005) Toxic Relationships and Adrenal Fatigue Can Often Be A Will Power Struggle. Body, Mind, Nutrition.

Retrieved from:
<https://www.drlam.com/articles/adrenal_fatigue_and_tox ic_relationships.asp>

65 Lipton, Bruce Ph.D, (2007) The Biology of Belief: Unleashing the Power of Consciousness, Matter and Miracles pg 54-57, 185-188

67 Rosenthal, Michelle (2010). PTSD Professional Perspective: Emotional Freedom Technique

Retrieved from:
<http://www.healmyptsd.com/2010/04/ptsd-professional-perspective-emotional-freedom-technique.html

51 Saeed,K (2014) PTSD in the Aftermath of Narcissistic Abuse. Let Me Reach with Kim Saeed

Retrieved from: https://letmereach.com/2014/02/01/ptsd-in-the-aftermath-of-narcissistic-abuse/

77 Saeed, Kim (2016) Top 8 Essential oils for emotional healing. Let me Reach with Kim Saeed.

Retrieved from: https://letmereach.com/2016/03/21/the-top-8-essential-oils-for-emotional-healing/

MY SOULMATE MY LOVE MY NARCISSIST

I love watching the facial expressions of the crème de le crème in the field of psychiatry and science worldwide as they begin to understand how profound quantum modalities are for the success in a client's healing process.

Nothing can be more rewarding.

There are so many who can use this knowledge.

My life experiences in conjunction with science has allowed me to write this book. Thank you for sharing it with others.

Dr. Bindu Babu

——————————————————I-M D, P H D

www.BinduBabu.com

Made in the USA
Coppell, TX
31 May 2021